Cocktails

AGRICOLA

COOKBOOK

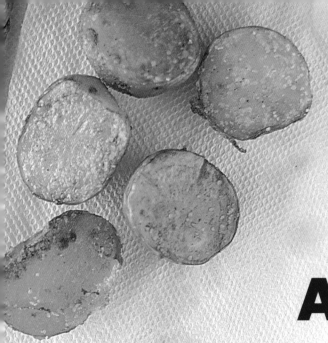

AGRICOLA
COOKBOOK

Seasonal American Comfort Food with Style and Grace

JOSH THOMSEN   KATE WINSLOW   STEVEN TOMLINSON

Photographs by GUY AMBROSINO

BURGESS LEA PRESS 2015

Agricola Cookbook : Thank a Farmer
Josh Thomsen, Kate Winslow, Steven Tomlinson

BLP

Burgess Lea Press
New Hope, Pennsylvania

www.burgessleapress.com

1 2 3 4 5 6 7 8 9 10
Printed in China by 1010 Printing Group Limited

Distributed in the United States by Simon & Schuster
Distributed in Canada by Simon & Schuster

Book design by Shubhani Sarkar
Cover design by Whitney Cookman
Photography by Guy Ambrosino
Agricola logo courtesy of Mucca Design

ISBN: 978-1-941868-00-3
Library of Congress Control Number:
2014954376

Burgess Lea Press donates 100 percent of our
after-tax profits on each book to culinary education,
feeding the hungry, farmland preservation and
other food-related causes.

CONTENTS

EATING ON
NATURE'S SCHEDULE

When my wife and I set out to develop and farm 112 acres outside Princeton, New Jersey, and, in turn, to create Agricola, I did not fully comprehend what I was about to undertake. I envisioned Great Road Farm supplying the needs of the restaurant, the two enterprises separated by a mere four miles on a grand old winding road that leads from town to the countryside. And I hoped that Agricola (the name means "farmer" in Latin, and has special resonance for me) would become a warm, welcoming place for the Princeton community to gather and eat.

Making a commitment to local, seasonal ingredients is not easy. It takes considerable effort and discipline to stick to what is in season in central New Jersey, and to write an appealing menu based on what the farmer provides, rather than what the industrial food system delivers. Doing this day after day is harder than I had ever imagined. But I believe this challenging path leads to the best flavor and the deepest authenticity.

Seasons and regions have mattered little to the food supply in our supermarkets today, and we are challenged daily by old habits and the plethora of choices around us. In a world in which food is so often seen as entertainment, the simple act of feeding guests can become lost. Agricola was designed and is operated with that age-old practice always in mind. In our comfortable dining rooms and welcoming bar, diners can slow down, relax, laugh deeply with friends over a good meal. Since we opened our doors on Witherspoon Street in 2013, I am proud to see that Agricola has become a true gathering place for our Princeton community, which includes people from all over the world.

At the outset, I identified "delivering on taste" as Agricola's foremost business objective. I was, after all, opening a restaurant which needed to sustain itself through delicious food. The more I learned, the simpler the vision became. Exceptional taste would start with our agricultural practices on Great Road Farm and by partnering with like-minded purveyors. Years of man's ingenuity and industrial farming had compromised soil health and vegetable quality, but through organic practices, we would attempt to restore life to our patch of earth, in the hopes of producing vigorous, nutrient-rich vegetables for Agricola and our CSA (community supported agriculture) program, in which subscribers from town

pick up their weekly vegetable boxes at the restaurant. In turn, the chef and kitchen staff would create simple preparations that would celebrate these raw ingredients and convince our guests we knew our craft. Knowing the scale of our undertaking—farming and serving a fickle public on nature's schedule—I understood I needed a team with expertise, yes, but most importantly, passion.

In November, 2012, I met Steve Tomlinson, a young designer turned small-scale farmer. During our first meeting we stood looking out over a bare field that was headed into winter. With a large restaurant due to open the following spring, I asked him if he could plan, schedule, plant, harvest and deliver great vegetables. He assured me that he could, and I'm happy to say that Great Road Farm does grow spectacular tomatoes, kale, turnips, peppers, cabbages, greens, garlic, carrots, and so much more, with ever more interesting varieties planned every year. But in addition, Steve's total commitment to sustainable and organic practices has pushed the restaurant to demand and expect more from all our purveyors. I am grateful to him for educating us and holding us all to the highest standards.

When chef Josh Thomsen and I met, he was already considering a return to his roots. A native New Jerseyan, Josh had lived and worked on the west coast since graduating from the Culinary Institute of America twenty years earlier. We immediately connected over the concept of simple food in which the supporting actors—robust, locally grown vegetables—might steal the show, making scallops from New Jersey waters or local chicken sing. Our partnership was forged in the hours we spent together in the lead-up to Agricola's opening, surviving and thriving through unexpected delays. And when we did finally open, I quickly came to appreciate how Josh's love for the craziness of operating a new kitchen (one might say his addiction to it!) made Agricola an instant success in Princeton.

This cookbook shares a bit of what we do and how we do it, from the ground up. I hope it finds a welcome place in your kitchen, just as there is always a table for you at Agricola.

JIM NAWN
Agricola Proprietor

A GARDEN STATE REVIVAL

When I left the East Coast to work as a chef in California, many of the large farms that surrounded my family's home in northern New Jersey had been sold off, making room for housing developments and corporate headquarters. The Garden State seemed like an idea that appeared only on license plates, its original meaning disappearing in a cloud of construction dust. But still, during those years when I had all of California's bounty to play with, I found myself longing for certain flavors that I remembered from my childhood—sugary sweet corn on the cob; the bracing tang of plump scallops from cold Atlantic waters; and, of course, ruby and garnet–hued tomatoes that are, for me, exactly what a sun-streaked August afternoon should taste like.

When Jim Nawn approached me about opening Agricola, I was thrilled to get into the kitchen with these ingredients again. Those tomatoes and corn were just as delicious as I remembered them, if not more so, thanks to the work of the small farmers who have put down roots in the area and are planting organically and biodynamically. But perhaps even more exciting was sampling some of the other, some might say less sexy, vegetables that Great Road Farm's Steve Tomlinson is growing—the many varieties of kales, radishes, beets, winter squash, turnips and more, all of them bursting with flavor.

Agricola's culinary philosophy is simple: Good food depends almost entirely on good ingredients. All of my favorite dishes are those based on the fewest ingredients at their peak of freshness. Because the food we create at Agricola is straightforward and unfussy, every component must be the best of its kind. I love the smell of freshly roasted vegetables right from our wood-fired oven, the look of a juicy steak cooking on the grill and the flavor of a whole roasted chicken showered with freshly picked herbs. In addition to Steve's fine work at Great Road Farm, I have been happy to collaborate with central New Jersey's vibrant network of fruit and vegetable farmers, cheesemakers, hog farmers, bee keepers, coffee roasters and distillers. The farmers, ranchers and fishermen you meet in this book are digging in and working hard to return Jersey to its Garden State glory.

Of course, writing a menu in September—when Steve is delivering everything from summery Indigo Rose tomatoes and shishito peppers to autumn's first delicata and kabocha squashes—is fun, no doubt about it. But mapping out the restaurant's dishes in February, when a wide variety of fresh, local produce is not available, is just as exciting, as my chef de cuisine Manlee Siu and I puzzle out how best to use our storage and cold-frame vegetables. It's a creative challenge, one that I think proves the merits of a good chef.

My favorite area of Agricola's dining room is the back wall of preserves. This colorful, every-changing collection of jars is not just for show—during dinner, you'll often see a server reach up to grab an extra jar of tomato sauce or pickled fennel that's needed in the kitchen. For those of us who live where the growing season is relatively short, preserving is a great way to enjoy the past season's bounty. We have no favorites—we pickle and ferment everything Mother Nature and Great Road Farm gives us. Zucchini and yellow squash, cabbages, ramps, turnips, beans, mushrooms, grapes, onions, tomatoes...these morsels show up all over Agricola's menu, in salads, on our burgers, as part of our cheeseboard and starring in our much-loved pickled and fermented plate.

I am so proud of the work we are doing at Agricola. Honest ingredients, combined sensibly and cooked properly, are the reasons why our food tastes so good and why we have struck a nerve within our community. Who says you can't go home again?

JOSH THOMSEN
Executive Chef

THE RHYTHM
OF THE SEASONS

Walking out into the field at Great Road Farm to check on newly planted crops brings out the parent in me. My wife and I recently had a baby boy, and the experience of becoming a father has reaffirmed my belief that producing healthy vegetables is essential to our family and our community. Nurturing plants from seed to harvest requires a lifecycle of care, but it all starts with healthy soil.

At Great Road Farm, what we don't do is just as important as what we do. For example, we do not spray our crops with anything. We do not use pesticides, herbicides or chemical fertilizers. What we do is use cover crops to build organic matter in the soil and to make nutrients available for our vegetable crops. Using plants to help grow more plants—what a concept! Rotating crops, so the same vegetables are not planted in the same place year after year, helps with pest control and wards off disease. These methods have been around for hundreds of years, and they create soil that is teeming with life. Healthy soil yields abundant harvests of nutrient rich food, which in turn allows the best flavor of our vegetables to shine through.

Season after season, intuition begins to guide us. Direct observation of storm clouds in the distance is a better indicator of rain then the weather report. Our farm is buffered by the Sourland Mountains and it seems we are resting on a rich glacial deposit because our soil is a well-drained loam. Patience, observation, and adjustment make us a better farm each year because we are constantly improving our relationship with the land.

The rhythm of the seasons sets the tone for planning, harvesting and partnering with Agricola. At the height of the season, while working out in the field, I take phone calls from the chefs, adding to the long vegetable order requested for the next day's delivery. In the wintertime we review the successes and failures of our past season to improve the flow between the farm and restaurant. Every year builds on the one before, yielding exciting possibilities that can appear spontaneously—like letting the dill plants go to seed and then saving those seeds to season our own pickles.

The farm and the restaurant have infinite variables: A bumper crop of Napa cabbage will get turned into kimchi, while a failed cauliflower harvest means we'll have to rely on another local supplier. Understanding what our farm can grow efficiently and what is too much for us to take on creates an opportunity to form relationships with neighboring farms and to pull resources from them (and vice versa). This helpful back-and-forth was once how communities worked, and it is exciting to see a resurgence of that spirit, as illustrated by the growing list of area farms cited on Agricola's menu.

My great-great-grandparents were hog farmers, and my grandparents were avid vegetable gardeners. I take comfort in the fact that I am carrying on a tradition of farming and community. I look forward to watching my son grow up on the farm, chasing chickens, getting lost in the weeds, pulling fresh vegetables from the ground. My goal is to teach him to respect the land and have a deep appreciation for the adventure of farming. After all, we are all connected in this web of life and must take care of each and every living thing.

STEVEN TOMLINSON
Farmer, Great Road Farm

FIRST COURSES

SOUPS & SMALLER PLATES

ROASTED BEET TARTARE WITH CRISPY ONION PETALS

SERVES 4

3 medium red beets

2 tablespoons extra-virgin olive oil

Kosher salt and freshly ground black pepper

2½ cups all-purpose flour, divided

½ cup cornstarch

1¾ cups ice-cold club soda

Canola oil, for frying

2 large Vidalia onions

2 radishes, preferably watermelon radishes, thinly sliced

2 tablespoons minced chives

Josh came up with this dish for a dinner he cooked at the James Beard House in New York City, as a way to showcase the produce of Great Road Farm. Seasoned only with olive oil, salt and pepper, the roasted beet tartare is dead simple to make. For a neat presentation, pack the tartare into a ⅓-cup measuring cup or ramekin and gently unmold it onto the plate. Or, for an appetizer that's easy to pass around at a party, top each onion petal with a small scoop of tartare.

Preheat the oven to 400°F. Wash and lightly scrub the beets, then pat dry and place on a sheet of foil. Drizzle with 1 tablespoon olive oil and season well with salt and pepper. Wrap the foil tightly around the beets and roast until tender, about 45 minutes.

While the beets are still warm, carefully peel and discard the skins. Place the beets in a food processor, adding a little of the roasting liquid left in the foil. Pulse 10 times, scraping down the sides with a rubber spatula, until the beets are finely chopped but still have some texture. Season with salt and pepper, and the remaining 1 tablespoon olive oil. Set aside.

In a large mixing bowl, combine 1½ cups flour, cornstarch and 1½ teaspoons salt. Gradually add the club soda, whisking constantly to make a smooth batter. Put the remaining 1 cup flour in a shallow bowl.

Heat at least 3 inches of canola oil to 350°F in a deep fryer or large saucepan with high sides. Peel the onions and cut into wedges. Separate the layers, saving the smaller layers for another use. Dredge the petals in the flour, then lightly coat in the batter. Working in batches, fry until golden brown and crisp, about 4 minutes. Drain the onion petals on paper towels and season with salt.

To serve, place a pile of beet tartare on one side of a plate and a pile of crispy onion petals on the other side. Sprinkle the radish slices and chives over the onions and serve.

Plan to make this soup the day you buy the peas (which is hopefully the same day they were picked). Peas start to convert their sugars into starch very quickly, and you want them to be at their sweet and tender best.

Prepare a small ice water bath. Heat the butter and olive oil in a pot over moderate heat. When the butter is foaming, add the onion, reduce the heat to low, and cook slowly, stirring occasionally, until the onion is translucent and very tender, 5 to 10 minutes. (Don't allow the onion to brown; it will discolor the soup.)

Add the stock, honey, salt and white pepper, and bring to a boil. Boil for 5 minutes. Increase the heat to high, add the peas, and boil rapidly for 2 minutes, or until the peas are tender. Remove from the heat. Transfer about ¼ cup of the peas to the ice water bath to stop the cooking process, then drain on paper towels. Set aside for garnishing.

Purée the remaining soup until smooth, either with an immersion blender or carefully working in batches in a blender. Strain the purée through a fine-mesh sieve into a large bowl. Set the bowl in an ice bath; cooling the soup quickly helps it retain its beautiful green color. When completely chilled, taste and adjust the seasonings. Ladle into small bowls and garnish with the reserved peas.

CHILLED SWEET PEA SOUP

SERVES 4

3 tablespoons unsalted butter
1 tablespoon extra-virgin olive oil
1 cup finely chopped white onions
4 cups Vegetable Stock (page 194)
2 tablespoons honey
2 teaspoons kosher salt
¼ teaspoon freshly ground white pepper
7 cups shelled fresh peas (from about 5 pounds peas in their pods)

CARROT GINGER SOUP

SERVES 4

FOR THE GINGER OIL:

1 cup canola oil
2 tablespoons ground ginger
1½ tablespoons ground
    turmeric

FOR THE LIME CRÈME
FRAÎCHE:

1 lime
¼ cup crème fraîche
1 tablespoon minced cilantro
    leaves
Kosher salt

FOR THE SOUP:

3 tablespoons extra-virgin
    olive oil
2 tablespoons Ginger Oil, plus
    more for garnishing
2 white onions, thinly sliced
2 small jalapeños, seeded and
    thinly sliced
2 small garlic cloves, minced
2 teaspoons finely grated fresh
    ginger
2 pounds carrots, sliced
8 cups Vegetable Stock
    (page 194)
Kosher salt

Our guests at Agricola are happy when chef de cuisine Manlee Siu makes this soup. The combination of sweet carrots, ginger and lime is a classic one, but this clean, simple presentation tastes very fresh. The ginger oil takes only minutes to make, but it does need to be prepared a day ahead, so plan accordingly.

To make the ginger oil, whisk together the canola oil, ground ginger and turmeric in a small saucepan. Bring to a simmer over moderate heat, then remove from the heat. Transfer the oil to a bowl and refrigerate overnight.

The following day, line a fine-mesh sieve with a dampened paper towel and strain the ginger oil into an airtight container. (Take care when pouring the oil; the turmeric can stain.) Store in the refrigerator until needed.

To make the lime crème fraîche, finely grate the zest of the lime into a small bowl, then juice the lime, adding the juice to the bowl. Whisk in the crème fraîche and cilantro and season with salt. Refrigerate until needed.

To make the soup, heat the olive oil and 2 tablespoons ginger oil in a saucepan over moderate heat. Add the onions, jalapeños, garlic and grated ginger and cook gently until translucent, about 5 minutes; do not let brown. Add the carrots and cook for 5 minutes. Add 6 cups vegetable stock and simmer until the carrots are tender, 20 to 30 minutes. Transfer the soup to a blender and purée until smooth. Strain through a fine-mesh sieve into a clean saucepan. Reheat the soup, thinning it with the remaining 2 cups stock, as needed, and season with salt.

To serve, ladle the soup into warm bowls, drizzle with ginger oil and top with a dollop of lime crème fraîche.

Underneath a celery root's surface dirt and gnarled skin lie cream-colored flesh and a pungent flavor—similar to bunch celery, but deeper and more sophisticated. Celeriac, as it's also known, has long been the star of céleri rémoulade, and it makes an incredibly silky soup. This version gets extra sweetness from pear peels; the fruit, glazed with honey, serves as a garnish.

Combine the diced pears and honey in a small sauté pan over moderately high heat and cook, stirring occasionally, until the pears are glazed, amber-colored and tender, about 5 minutes. Remove from the heat and set aside.

Melt 3 tablespoons of the butter in a large heavy pot over moderate heat. Add the onions, leeks, celery and garlic and cook, stirring occasionally, until softened but not browned, 6 to 8 minutes. Add the celery root, potato, vegetable stock and the reserved pear skins. Bring to a boil, then reduce the heat and simmer gently, covered, until the vegetables are tender, about 30 minutes.

Working in batches, purée the mixture in a blender until thick and smooth (use caution when blending hot liquids). Add the remaining 3 tablespoons butter and blend until smooth. Transfer the soup to a clean pot, and season to taste with salt and white pepper. Keep warm.

Ladle the soup into warm bowls and garnish each with a spoonful of the honeyed pears.

CELERY ROOT SOUP WITH HONEYED PEARS

SERVES 4 TO 6

3 ripe but firm pears, peeled (peels reserved), cored, and diced into ½-inch pieces
2 tablespoons honey
6 tablespoons unsalted butter
1 white onion, sliced
1 leek, white part only, thinly sliced
2 celery ribs, sliced
3 garlic cloves, minced

1 large celery root (about 1½ pounds), peeled and diced
1 medium russet potato, peeled and diced
8 cups Vegetable Stock (page 194)
Kosher salt and freshly ground white pepper

TASSOT APIARIES

Tucked in a housing development above the town of Milford, New Jersey, Buzzing Acres Farm is the home of Tassot Apiaries. The Tassots' honeycomb is essential to our cheeseboard, and we also love their honey sticks, a fun way to sweeten hot tea.

An understated sign leads to a small wooden barn where Jean-Claude Tassot and his wife Bea harvest honey, lead workshops and sell their wildflower, buckwheat and linden honeys, as well as honeycomb, pollen, and candles.

It's not where you'd expect a life-or-death operation to be taking place, but in a sense, that's exactly what is happening on these 10 acres. About one-third of everything we eat, as Jean-Claude points out, is a direct result of the work of honeybees.

Honeybee pollination is essential to the propagation of herbs, wildflowers, trees, fruits and vegetables. It's a mutually beneficial relationship: plants produce more abundant fruits when pollinated by bees, and bees make gorgeous honey from a varied diet of healthy plants.

Jean-Claude started keeping bees as a child in Burgundy, and when he and Bea moved to New Jersey, they had a hard time finding local honey produced without chemicals. So he started raising bees again: once again, home is where the hive is.

MUSHROOM SOUP WITH ROASTED CIPOLLINI ONIONS

SERVES 4

6 cipollini onions or shallots, unpeeled
3 tablespoons unsalted butter
Pinch of curry powder
Kosher salt
¼ cup extra-virgin olive oil
6 sprigs fresh sage
3 sprigs fresh rosemary
2 medium yellow onions, thinly sliced
3 garlic cloves, minced

Freshly ground white pepper
1½ pounds mixed fresh mushrooms, such as oyster, shiitake, porcini and cremini, sliced
9 cups Mushroom Stock (page 194)
1½ cups heavy cream
1 tablespoon finely chopped chives

This velvety purée packs an intense mushroom punch. We get all of our mushrooms from our friend Alan Kaufman at Shibumi Farm, but wherever you shop for mushrooms, seek out the freshest ones you can find—they should be firm, never soggy.

Preheat the oven to 400°F. Place the cipollini onions in the middle of a large square of aluminum foil, add 1 tablespoon butter, sprinkle with the curry powder and season with salt. Fold the foil to form a pouch around the onions and roast until tender, 15 to 18 minutes. When cool enough to handle, carefully peel the onions and chop into bite-sized pieces. Set aside.

Heat the oil in a large heavy pot over moderate heat. Tie the sprigs of sage and rosemary together with kitchen twine. When the oil is hot add the herb bundle and cook until sizzling and fragrant, about 1 minute. Add the yellow onions, garlic, 1½ teaspoons salt and ¼ teaspoon white pepper and cook until the onions are softened and translucent, about 5 minutes. Increase the heat to high and add the mushrooms. Cook, stirring occasionally, until the mushrooms release their liquid and start to caramelize, about 10 minutes.

Add the mushroom stock, then reduce the heat to moderate and simmer for 30 minutes. Pluck out the herb bundle and discard it. Stir in the cream and remaining 2 tablespoons butter. Remove from the heat and purée the soup until smooth, either with an immersion blender or carefully working in batches in a blender. Strain the soup through a fine-mesh sieve into a clean pot. Season to taste with salt and pepper.

To serve, ladle the soup into 4 warm soup bowls and garnish with the roasted cipollini onions and chopped chives.

GOAT CHEESE–POTATO TERRINE WITH BABY BEETS AND BALSAMIC SYRUP

SERVES ABOUT 20

FOR THE TERRINE:

2½ pounds goat cheese
  (we use Coach Farm)
½ cup finely chopped chives
3 large russet potatoes
½ cup clarified butter
Kosher salt and freshly ground
  black pepper

FOR THE BEETS:

4 to 5 pounds baby beets (40 to
  50 loose beets), preferably
  a mix of purple, golden and
  striped varieties
½ cup plus 3 tablespoons
  extra-virgin olive oil
12 sprigs fresh thyme
Kosher salt and freshly ground
  black pepper
¼ cup freshly squeezed lemon
  juice
3 tablespoons finely chopped
  chives

FOR THE BALSAMIC SYRUP:

3 cups balsamic vinegar
4 fresh thyme sprigs

TO ASSEMBLE AND SERVE:

Micro arugula
Extra-virgin olive oil

One of our showstoppers—layers of creamy goat cheese and paper-thin strips of potato are seared and served with a drizzle of rich balsamic syrup and a salad of baby beets from Great Road Farm. It requires a bit of work, yes, but each step is very straightforward.

Obviously, this recipe is designed for a crowd. If you aren't planning to serve so many people, the terrine and balsamic syrup will keep for up to a week in the refrigerator; simply scale down the number of beets accordingly. That said, we're always happy to have extra roasted beets on hand in the fridge, ready to be added to salads or warmed up as a side dish.

To make the terrine, preheat the oven to 300°F. Line a baking sheet with a silicone baking mat or a piece of parchment paper.

Mix together the goat cheese and chives in a bowl and set aside. (It is helpful to divide the goat cheese mixture into 4 equal portions of about 10 ounces each, so the layers will all be the same.)

Peel the potatoes and, using a mandoline, cut them lengthwise into 1/16-inch-thick slices. Working in batches, dip the potato slices in the clarified butter and place on the lined baking sheet. Season the potatoes with salt and pepper then top with another silicone baking mat or a piece of parchment (this will keep the potatoes from curling as they cook). Bake until the potatoes are just cooked through but still pliable, 5 to 7 minutes. Transfer the potatoes to a tray and let cool. Repeat with the remaining potatoes.

Line a 10 × 3–inch terrine mold with plastic wrap. Arrange overlapping potato slices along the bottom of the terrine and then up the sides, using enough potatoes to hang over the edge

[CONTINUED]

of the terrine. Fill the potato-lined terrine with one quarter of the goat cheese mixture, packing it in firmly. Add a layer of potatoes, then another layer of goat cheese; repeat until all the cheese has been used. Flip the overhanging potato slices over the goat cheese mixture, cover with plastic wrap, and refrigerate for 24 hours.

To make the beets, preheat the oven to 400°F. Toss the beets with ½ cup olive oil and the thyme sprigs and season with salt and pepper. Wrap the beets and thyme in aluminum foil and roast until tender, 30 to 45 minutes. When cool enough to handle, peel and cut the beets into wedges. Toss with the lemon juice, chives and remaining 3 tablespoons oil. Season with salt and pepper. Set aside.

To make the balsamic syrup, combine the vinegar and thyme in a saucepan and bring to a simmer over moderate heat. Continue to simmer until the mixture is thick enough to coat the back of a wooden spoon and has reduced to about 1½ cups, 30 to 45 minutes. Strain the mixture through a fine-mesh sieve into a bowl and let cool.

To assemble and serve, turn the terrine out onto a cutting board, remove the plastic wrap, and cut into ½-inch-thick slices and season with black pepper. Heat a nonstick sauté pan over high heat and, working in batches, sear the terrine slices until golden brown, about 12 seconds. Flip on to room temperature plates (browned side face up). Arrange the beet salad next to the terrine and top with the micro arugula. Drizzle a circle of olive oil around the terrine and beets, followed by a drizzle of the balsamic syrup.

ATLANTIC COD FRITTERS WITH SHAVED FENNEL SALAD

When shopping for salt cod, look for snow-white, meaty center cuts, rather than thin tail pieces. As the cod soaks, taste it often—it's ready to use when it tastes fresh and well seasoned, not briny.

SERVES 6

FOR THE FRITTERS:

8 ounces skinless, boneless salt cod
1½ pounds russet potatoes
2 cups whole milk, or as needed
5 cloves roasted garlic, chopped into a paste
Pinch of sweet paprika
1 cup extra-virgin olive oil
Kosher salt and freshly ground white pepper
1 cup all-purpose flour
6 tablespoons cornstarch
1 tablespoon baking powder
1 teaspoon fine sea salt
1 cup beer, preferably a light ale, or sparkling water
Vegetable oil, for frying

FOR THE SHAVED FENNEL SALAD:

1 large fennel bulb, very thinly sliced (preferably on a mandolin)
¼ cup roughly chopped Oven-Dried Tomatoes (page 193)
2 tablespoons torn flat-leaf parsley leaves
1 tablespoon extra-virgin olive oil
Kosher salt
Fennel pollen, for garnish

To make the fritters, cut the salt cod into big chunks and rinse well. Place the cod in a bowl and cover with cold water by two inches and soak, refrigerated. Change the water every 8 hours. The cod is ready to be used when it feels like fresh fish again and tastes well seasoned but not overly salty. This may take anywhere from 12 to 48 hours.

Preheat the oven to 400°F. Prick the potatoes all over with a fork, place on a sheet pan and bake until very tender, 45 to 60 minutes.

Remove the cod from the water, rinse it, and place it in a saucepan with 2 cups milk or enough to cover it. When the potatoes are finished baking, start heating the milk and cod over moderately low heat and gently poach the fish until tender, flaky and no longer translucent, 5 to 10 minutes. Remove from the heat.

Halve the potatoes, scoop out the flesh, and press it through a fine-mesh sieve or the finest disk of a food mill. Cover the potatoes with plastic wrap and keep warm.

Drain the poached cod and discard the milk. Put the cod in a food processor and pulse briefly, just enough to break it up. Add the roasted garlic and paprika and pulse a few times. Add ¾ cup of the olive oil in 3 batches and pulse to combine, scraping down the sides of the processor after each addition.

Transfer the processed cod to a large bowl and fold in half of the warm potatoes. Taste as you add the rest of the potatoes, ¼ cup at a time, ensuring that you can still taste the cod. Add a few more tablespoons of olive oil, just enough to provide a balance of cod, potato and olive oil, then season to taste with kosher salt and white pepper. Roll the mixture into 18 balls, about 2 tablespoons each, and set aside.

Whisk together the flour, cornstarch, baking powder and sea salt, then add the beer and mix to get a thick, slightly lumpy batter. Let sit for at least 10 minutes. If the mixture seems too thick after sitting, add a few more tablespoons of beer to thin it.

Heat at least 3 inches of oil to 350°F in a deep fryer or large saucepan with high sides. Working in batches, dip 6 cod balls in the batter, then drop carefully into the hot oil. Turn the balls to brown all sides evenly, 3 to 4 minutes per batch. Using a slotted spoon, transfer the fritters to drain on paper towels. Continue with the remaining cod balls.

To make the fennel salad, combine the fennel, tomatoes, parsley and olive oil in a bowl and season to taste with salt. Arrange the fennel salad on 6 small plates, top each with 3 fritters and sprinkle with the fennel pollen.

In the spring, shad move from the sea to coastal rivers to spawn, and it is during these short weeks that we can enjoy shad roe, one of North America's great delicacies. Look for creamy, fresh-looking, sweet-smelling lobes; their color will range from yellowish red to deep red. The roe's outer membrane should already be removed for you. If you are lucky enough to live somewhere where you can catch your own shad, remove this outer membrane carefully, so as not to damage the thin inner membrane that protects the delicate eggs.

Preheat the oven to 350°F. Cut the bacon crosswise into ½-inch pieces. Cook the bacon in a small sauté pan over moderate heat, stirring occasionally, until crisp and browned, 8 to 10 minutes. Using a slotted spoon, transfer the bacon to paper towels to drain. Set aside.

If necessary, trim the shad roe by removing the excess membrane that holds the pair together and any veins. Wash the roe very gently. Pat dry and season with salt and pepper.

Heat 6 tablespoons butter in a medium sauté pan over moderately low heat. When the butter has melted, place the shad roe in the pan; if the butter is not nearly covering the lobes, add a little more.

Place the pan in the preheated oven and roast until the shad roe is firm, 10 to 15 minutes. Check the roe at around 10 minutes by gently squeezing it at the thickest part to feel for firmness. If it is still soft, cook a little longer.

When the roe is done, divide it between 4 warm plates. Pour off about half of the butter and heat the remaining butter over moderate heat until it begins to brown and develop a nutty aroma (watch out for the popping of a few roe that may remain in the pan). When the butter is well browned, quickly stir in the reserved bacon, anchovies, parsley, capers and lemon juice.

Spoon the seasoned browned butter over the roe and serve immediately with toasted baguette slices.

SLOW-ROASTED SHAD ROE WITH BROWN BUTTER, CAPERS, BACON AND LEMON

SERVES 4

2 strips smoked bacon

2 pairs of shad roe, about 6 ounces each

Kosher salt and freshly ground black pepper

6 to 8 tablespoons unsalted butter

2 anchovy filets, finely chopped

2 tablespoons chopped flat-leaf parsley leaves

1 tablespoon capers, rinsed and chopped

Juice of 1 lemon

8 slices of baguette, toasted

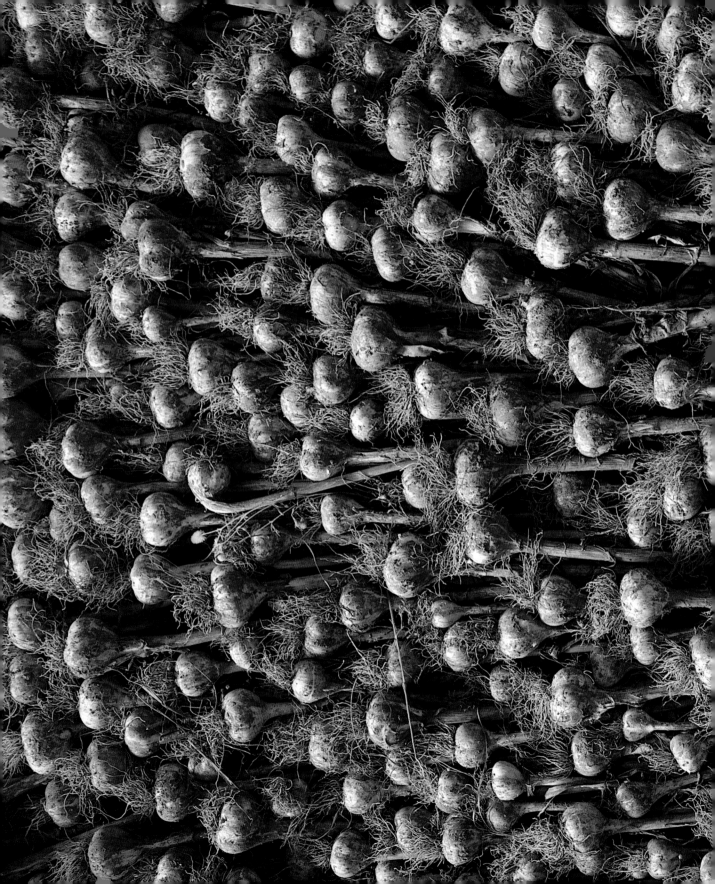

Roasted Garlic: Concentrating Goodness

Several of our recipes call for cloves of roasted garlic, which offer a sweeter, mellower depth than raw garlic does. While roasted garlic adds backbone to our Almond Hummus (page 38) and Atlantic Cod Fritters (page 18), it's also delicious simply smeared on country bread and drizzled with olive oil, mashed into potatoes or added to a flat-bread topping.

To make your own roasted garlic, strip off the papery outer skin from a head of garlic (do not separate the cloves). Put the garlic on a square of aluminum foil, drizzle with some olive oil, then wrap the garlic in foil. Roast the garlic in a preheated 350°F oven until soft, 40 to 50 minutes. Let the garlic cool slightly before squeezing out the roasted cloves. If you don't use all the cloves at once, pop them in an airtight container. They will keep, refrigerated, for about a week.

THE PERFECT CRAB CAKE

SERVES 4

FOR THE CRAB CAKES:

½ cup mayonnaise

1 large egg, lightly beaten

1 tablespoon Dijon mustard

1 tablespoon Worcestershire
　sauce

½ teaspoon hot sauce, such as
　Tabasco

Finely grated zest of 1 lemon

1 pound jumbo lump crab
　meat, picked over

½ cup panko, finely crushed

¼ cup canola oil

FOR THE CARROT PURÉE:

2 carrots, chopped

1 tablespoon butter

Kosher salt and freshly ground
　black pepper

FOR THE SALAD:

½ cup sugar snap peas,
　trimmed

3 carrots, preferably a mixture
　of colors, cut into thin
　matchsticks

2 radishes, thinly sliced

1 tablespoon extra-virgin
　olive oil

1 tablespoon Sherry vinegar

Kosher salt and freshly ground
　black pepper

Only six months after opening, we were honored to have this dish chosen for the cover of New Jersey Monthly magazine's 2013 restaurant issue, which named us a top restaurant in the state. Use a gentle hand when mixing and forming these crab cakes; you'll be rewarded with a tender cake that tastes of pure, sweet crab. We often serve bite-sized versions at parties at the restaurant. Instead of making eight large cakes, divide the mixture into two dozen donut hole–sized ones.

To make the crab cakes, whisk together, the mayonnaise, egg, mustard, Worcestershire sauce, hot sauce and lemon zest in a small bowl until smooth.

In a medium bowl, gently toss the crabmeat with the panko. Gently fold the mayonnaise mixture into the crabmeat. Cover and refrigerate for at least 1 hour.

To make the carrot purée, put the carrots in a saucepan and cover with water. Bring to a boil then reduce heat and simmer until tender, 8 to 10 minutes. Drain the carrots, reserving some of the cooking liquid, and transfer to a blender with the butter. Blend until smooth, adding a little of the cooking liquid if needed to thin the purée, and season to taste with salt and pepper. Set aside.

To make the salad, prepare a small ice water bath. Cook the sugar snap peas in a small pot of boiling water until crisp-tender, about 2 minutes. Drain and transfer to the ice water bath. Drain the cooled peas well and pat dry with paper towels. Cut the peas in half on the diagonal.

Combine the carrots, radishes and snap peas in a bowl and toss with the olive oil and vinegar. Season to taste with salt and pepper.

Scoop the crab mixture into eight ⅓-cup mounds; lightly pack into patties, about 1½ inches thick.

Heat the canola oil in a large sauté pan over moderately high heat until shimmering. Add the crab cakes and cook until deeply golden and heated through, 2 to 3 minutes per side.

Make a pool of carrot purée on 4 plates and drag the back of a spoon through the purée to streak the plate. Arrange 2 crab cakes on each plate, next to the carrot streak. Top the crab cakes with the vegetable salad and serve.

Soft-shell lovers spend the year waiting for those precious few spring weeks when Atlantic blue crabs molt in preparation for growing new shells. We like to pair this all-American delicacy with the best vegetables of the moment: asparagus, ramps and tender black trumpet mushrooms. It's a true celebration of spring on the East Coast. If you're squeamish about cleaning the crabs yourself, ask your fishmonger to do it for you; just be prepared to cook any soft-shell crabs, alive or cleaned, the day you buy them.

MARYLAND SOFT-SHELL CRABS WITH SPRING VEGETABLES

SERVES 4

1 cup shelled fresh peas
3 tablespoons extra-virgin olive oil, divided
1 shallot, thinly sliced
Kosher salt
1 cup Vegetable Stock (page 194)
1 tablespoon chopped tarragon leaves
1 teaspoon chopped flat-leaf parsley leaves
Freshly ground black pepper
4 soft-shell crabs, cleaned

8 to 10 stalks green asparagus, trimmed and thinly sliced (about 1 cup)
1 cup black trumpet mushrooms, trimmed and sliced
1 medium carrot, finely diced
6 to 8 ramps, chopped into 1-inch pieces
1 tablespoon chopped chives
8 sprigs pea shoots
Lemon wedges, for serving

Prepare a small ice water bath. Cook the peas in a small pot of salted boiling water for 2 minutes. Drain the peas and transfer to the ice water bath to stop the cooking. When cool, drain well and set aside.

Heat 1 tablespoon olive oil in a small saucepan over moderate heat. Add the shallots, season with generous pinch of salt and cook, stirring occasionally, until tender, about 2 minutes. Add the vegetable stock and half of the blanched peas. Increase the heat to moderately high and cook the peas until tender, 2 to 3 minutes. Transfer the pea and shallot mixture to a blender, add the tarragon and parsley, and purée until smooth. Season to taste with salt and pepper. Set aside, covered, to keep warm.

Season the crabs all over with salt and pepper. Heat a large sauté pan over moderate heat and add 1 tablespoon olive oil. When it just starts to smoke, add the crabs to the pan and cook until golden brown, about 2 minutes per side. (Be careful while the crabs are frying; sometimes they pop and spray their hot juices.) Drain the crabs on paper towels, loosely covered with foil to keep warm.

Meanwhile, heat the remaining 1 tablespoon olive oil in a sauté pan over moderate heat. Add the asparagus, mushrooms, carrots and ramps and cook, stirring occasionally, until the vegetables are tender but not browned, 6 to 8 minutes. Stir in the reserved peas and cook just until heated through. Season to taste with salt and pepper.

To serve, spoon a circle of the pea purée in the middle of 4 plates. Add a small pile of the vegetables in the center of the purée then top with a crab. Garnish with the chopped chives and pea shoots and serve with lemon wedges.

POACHED SHRIMP WITH PICKLED WATERMELON AND GREEN GODDESS DRESSING

To make the pickled watermelon, combine the vinegar, water, sugar, salt and lemon in a large saucepan and bring to a boil over moderately high heat. Cook, stirring, until the sugar is completely dissolved. Remove from the heat and cool completely.

Using a sharp knife, cut the rind from the watermelon and discard. Cut the watermelon's red flesh into ½-inch cubes (you should have about 1 cup). Place the cubes in a vacuum seal bag, cover with the cooled brine, and seal on medium pressure. Once the bag is completely sealed, remove the watermelon, drain off the brine and set the pickle aside until ready to serve. If you don't have a vacuum sealer, combine the watermelon and brine in a bowl and refrigerate for at least 2 hours and up to 6 hours.

To make the shrimp, fill a large saucepan with 2½ quarts water. Add the garlic, bay leaves, lemon, salt, peppercorns and chili flakes and bring to a simmer over moderately high heat.

Meanwhile, clean the shrimp by running a small, sharp knife down the length of their backs, through the shells, and removing the dark vein. When the poaching liquid has come to a simmer, remove it from heat, and once it has stopped bubbling, add the shrimp. Let sit, off the heat, until the shrimp are cooked through and pink, 3 to 5 minutes. Use a slotted spoon to remove the shrimp and drain well. Refrigerate until cool, and then peel and discard the shells before serving. (Save the poaching liquid for another use, if you like.)

To make the dressing, combine the anchovy, lemon juice, lemon zest, sugar and mustard in a blender. With blender running, slowly pour in the grapeseed oil and blend until the dressing emulsifies. Season with salt and pepper and add the avocado, parsley, tarragon and chives and blend until the dressing is completely smooth, adding a little water if the dressing is too thick.

To serve, make small pools of green goddess dressing around the plate, top with the shrimp and watermelon and garnish with the radish sprouts, if you like.

Made with avocado and a variety of herbs, green goddess dressing is particularly well suited to the salads of summer. It's also very good alongside tender new potatoes or grilled fish.

Poaching the shrimp in hot, but not boiling, liquid is a nice technique that results in beautifully tender shrimp. Return the shells to the poaching liquid and continue to simmer for a few minutes to make a delicately flavored shrimp stock—a good base for a summery chowder or risotto.

SERVES 4

FOR THE PICKLED WATERMELON:

1 cup champagne vinegar
1 cup water
¼ cup sugar
¼ teaspoon kosher salt
½ lemon, sliced
8 ounces red seedless watermelon

FOR THE SHRIMP:

3 garlic cloves, peeled and crushed
2 bay leaves
1 lemon, halved
1 tablespoon kosher salt
1 teaspoon black peppercorns
¼ teaspoon dried red chili flakes
16 medium shell-on shrimp

FOR THE GREEN GODDESS DRESSING:

1 anchovy filet
1 tablespoon freshly squeezed lemon juice
½ teaspoon finely grated lemon zest
½ teaspoon sugar
¼ teaspoon Dijon mustard
¾ cup grapeseed oil
Kosher salt and freshly ground black pepper
½ avocado, pitted, peeled and cubed
2 tablespoons chopped flat-leaf parsley leaves
2 tablespoons chopped tarragon leaves
2 tablespoons chopped chives
Radish sprouts, for garnishing (optional)

SEARED FOIE GRAS WITH CARAMELIZED APPLES AND FRENCH TOAST

SERVES 4

Four 3-ounce slices of 1-inch thick, grade "A" foie gras
Kosher salt and freshly ground black pepper
1 Granny Smith apple, skin on
¼ cup granulated sugar
2 tablespoons unsalted butter, divided

1 large egg
3 tablespoons whole milk
½ vanilla bean
Two 1-inch-thick slices of brioche or challah bread, crusts removed and cut in half
1 tablespoon minced chives

The folks behind Hudson Valley Foie Gras, in upstate New York, have raised Moulard ducks and produced foie gras since 1982. They take tremendous care of their animals, and in turn, we take great care cooking their prized foie gras. Lightly scoring the liver allows the seasoning to penetrate and helps it look beautiful on the plate.

Using a sharp knife, lightly score both sides of the foie gras in a crosshatch manner. Season the foie gras all over with salt and pepper. Refrigerate until ready to sear.

Core the apple and cut it into 4 thick rings. Dredge the apple rings in the sugar. Heat 1 tablespoon butter in a sauté pan over moderately high heat. When the butter foams, add the apples and cook until golden brown and caramelized on both sides, about 4 minutes per side. Remove from the pan, set aside and keep warm.

Whisk together the egg and milk in a shallow bowl. Split the vanilla bean lengthwise and scrape the seeds into the mixture and whisk to combine. Add the bread and soak, flipping halfway through, until the liquid is absorbed, about 10 minutes.

Heat the remaining 1 tablespoon butter in the cleaned sauté pan over moderate heat. Add the soaked bread and cook until golden brown, about 5 minutes per side. Remove from the pan, set aside and keep warm.

Heat a sauté pan over high heat (do not add any oil or butter). Add the foie gras and cook until golden brown, about 2 minutes per side, taking care not to let it burn. Remove from the heat and drain the foie gras briefly on paper towels.

To serve, place the French toast on 4 warm plates. Top with the apples and foie gras and garnish with chives. Serve at once.

We love to pack individual servings of this creamy mousse into small mason jars at Agricola, and it's fun to do at home, too. It's practical, yet feels very special. Pair this rich mousse with a tart condiment like Cranberry Aigre-Doux (page 182).

Put the livers in a bowl and cover with the milk. Soak overnight in the refrigerator (this step helps to remove any impurities from the livers).

Drain the livers well and pat dry with paper towels. Place a large sauté pan over high heat. Add 2 tablespoons of the butter and the livers and cook, stirring occasionally, until browned, 1 to 2 minutes (the centers should still be pink).

Add the shallots and cook, stirring occasionally, until translucent, about 2 minutes. Season with salt then add the thyme, allspice and pepper and cook, stirring, until fragrant, about 30 seconds. Add the cognac and deglaze the pan, stirring and scraping the bottom of the pan to loosen any browned bits.

Remove from the heat and transfer the liver mixture to a blender or a food processor. Add the cream, and blend on high until thick and smooth. Add ½ cup of the melted butter and blend until combined.

Strain the liver mixture though a fine-mesh sieve into a bowl, pressing hard on the solids with a spatula, and let cool. Transfer the mousse to a crock or small (3-ounce) mason jars then pour the remaining ½ cup melted butter over the top of the mousse to make an airtight seal. Refrigerate for at least 2 hours before serving.

Serve the mousse with slices of toasted bread.

CHICKEN LIVER MOUSSE

SERVES 4 TO 6

2 cups fresh chicken livers (about 1 pound), trimmed and rinsed

5 cups whole milk

2 tablespoons unsalted butter, plus 1 cup (2 sticks) melted unsalted butter

2 tablespoons minced shallots

Kosher salt

1 tablespoon fresh thyme leaves

1 teaspoon ground allspice

1 teaspoon freshly ground black pepper

¼ cup cognac

¼ cup heavy cream

Toasted bread, for serving

BRAISED BEEF TONGUE WITH SALSA VERDE

SERVES 8 TO 10

1 fresh beef tongue (about 3 pounds)

1 cup white wine

4 garlic cloves

1 medium onion, chopped

4 fresh thyme sprigs

3 bay leaves

1 rosemary sprig

1 tablespoon black peppercorns

1 teaspoon dried red chili flakes

2 whole cloves

2 to 3 tablespoons extra-virgin olive oil

Kosher salt and freshly ground black pepper

Salsa Verde (page 32)

Watercress, for garnish (optional)

If you have never tried fresh tongue, you're missing something special—it's juicy and moist, with a robust, beefy flavor. Tongue is very popular among a range of cultures. Italians often add it to bollito misto. In Jewish delis, tongue is found smoked, sliced and stuffed into sandwiches. In Mexico, cooks make lengua tacos, folding the tender meat into corn tortillas. At Agricola, we first braise the tongue slowly in wine and herbs. Then we slice and pan-fry it, and drizzle the golden-brown meat with a bright salsa verde.

Place the tongue in a large pot with the white wine and about 12 cups cold water to cover. Bring to a boil, skim the foam from the top, and add the garlic, onion, thyme, bay leaves, rosemary, peppercorns, chili flakes and cloves. Reduce the heat to moderately low and simmer until tender (a roasting fork should very easily pierce the thickest part of the tongue), 2 to 3 hours.

Remove the tongue from the braising liquid, let cool slightly, then peel off the skin. Most of the skin should come off easily, just by using your fingers. If there are any places where it is difficult to remove, carefully trim it off with a knife. Using the edge of a sharp knife, scrape the surface of the tongue. Return the tongue to the braising liquid and let cool completely then refrigerate overnight.

Remove the tongue from the liquid and trim away any excess fat. Working straight down through the thick, back end, cut the tongue into ⅛-inch-thick slices. When you reach the thinner front portion, cut the tongue on the diagonal, also in ⅛-inch-thick slices.

Heat 1 tablespoon olive oil in a large sauté pan over high heat. Working in batches, season the slices of tongue with salt and pepper and add to pan. Cook until golden brown, about 1 minute per side. Repeat with the remaining tongue, using the remaining olive oil, as needed, to cook it.

To serve, arrange the seared tongue on a serving platter and drizzle with some of the salsa verde. Garnish with some watercress, if you like, and serve the remaining salsa verde on the side.

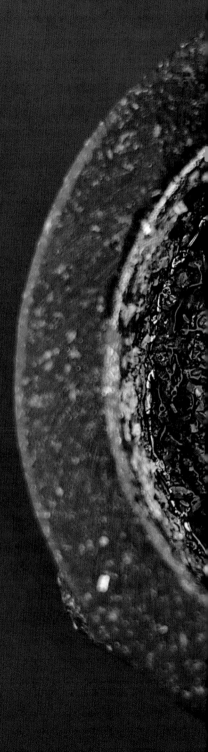

SALSA VERDE

This bright, herbaceous sauce is delicious with rich cuts of meat. Making salsa verde in a food processor or blender is certainly faster, but you miss out on the lovely, uneven texture that results from hand-chopping the herbs. Wait to stir in the lemon juice until just before serving; the acid will discolor the herbs if added too early.

MAKES ABOUT 1½ CUPS

3 anchovy fillets, finely chopped

2 tablespoons minced shallots

1 tablespoon capers, rinsed and finely chopped

1 tablespoon finely grated lemon zest

½ cup finely chopped flat-leaf parsley leaves

¼ cup finely chopped mint leaves

¼ cup finely chopped basil leaves

2 tablespoons finely chopped oregano leaves

¾ cup extra-virgin olive oil

Kosher salt and freshly ground black pepper

1 tablespoon freshly squeezed lemon juice

Using a mortar and pestle, pound the anchovies, shallots and capers to a paste. (If you don't have a mortar, chop and mash them together with the side of a heavy knife.) Stir in the lemon zest. Stir in the chopped herbs and the olive oil, and season with salt and pepper to taste. Let the salsa sit for 30 minutes or so for the flavors to develop. Just before serving, stir in the lemon juice, then taste again and adjust the seasonings.

SALADS

FROM FIELD & FARM

HEIRLOOM TOMATO SALAD WITH ALMOND HUMMUS AND COMPRESSED WATERMELON

SERVES 4

½ cup whole raw almonds (about 3 ounces)

1 cup extra-virgin olive oil, divided

1 clove roasted garlic

3 tablespoons freshly squeezed lemon juice

Kosher salt

Pinch of Aleppo pepper

½ cup packed whole basil leaves, plus 2 tablespoons torn basil leaves

1½ pounds watermelon

3 ripe heirloom tomatoes, cored and cut into wedges

Freshly ground black pepper

Nothing beats ripe Jersey tomatoes, and this salad really lets them shine. The almond hummus, inspired by one served at Josh's friend Amy Murray's Revival Kitchen in Berkeley, provides a nice foil to the acidity of the fruit. Compressed fruits and vegetables are a simple way to add dimension and concentrated flavor to any dish. If you don't have a vacuum sealer, this salad is still delicious with fresh, ripe watermelon.

To make the hummus, place the almonds in a bowl and cover with cold water. Soak overnight at room temperature.

Drain the almonds and slip their skins off with your fingers. Using a blender or food processor, purée the skinned almonds, ½ cup olive oil, roasted garlic, lemon juice, ½ teaspoon salt and Aleppo pepper until smooth. If the hummus seems too thick, add 1 tablespoon cold water at a time and process until you reach the desired consistency.

To make the basil oil, bring a medium pot of salted water to a boil. Prepare an ice bath. Put the whole basil leaves in a sieve and dip in the boiling water for 10 seconds. Drain the leaves and immediately transfer to the ice bath. Let the basil cool for a few minutes, then drain well and pat dry. Transfer to a blender. Add ¼ cup olive oil and process until smooth. Transfer to a bowl and set aside.

To make the compressed watermelon, cut off and discard the rind from the watermelon, then cut the flesh into 1-inch-thick slices. Remove any seeds. Place the watermelon slices into a vacuum bag. Place the bag into a vacuum sealer and seal at 100% power. Let sit in the bag for 2 hours, then remove and cut into 2 × 1 × ¼-inch pieces. Refrigerate until ready to use.

Toss the tomatoes in a large bowl with the torn basil leaves and the remaining ¼ cup olive oil. Season with salt and pepper.

To serve, make a pool of hummus on 4 salad plates. Drag the back of a spoon through the hummus, streaking it across each plate. Arrange the seasoned tomatoes and watermelon over the hummus and garnish with the basil oil.

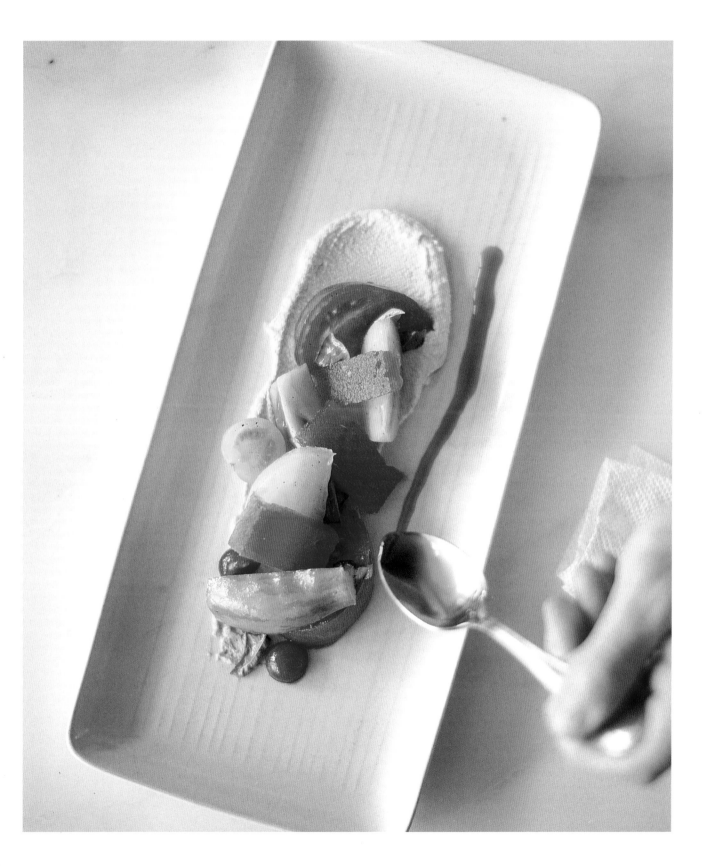

Tomatoes: Great Joy of a New Jersey Summer

Tomatoes in season are well worth waiting for. At Great Road Farm, we grow more than 60 varieties, from giant Pink Elephants to petite Green Grapes and Violet Jaspers. Between them, they display almost every tomato characteristic imaginable: spherical to pear-shaped; sweet to smoky; firm, peachy flesh to juicy drippiness.

We start seed in the greenhouse in April and transplant out to the field after the last frost date, May 15. Straw mulch helps to suppress weeds and prevent soil splash on the leaves when it rains. Tomatoes like fertile, well-composted soil, and thrive in warm, dry weather; wet, cool summers produce low yields and bland fruits.

Our first tomatoes are ready in the high tunnel around mid-July, and we keep picking every week until the first frost, which usually happens some time in mid-October. Most of the varieties we grow are open pollinated, which means we can save the seeds from year to year, with the same results. Many years ago, a neighbor passed down a tomato named the Corsalo to one of my mentors, Mike Rassweiler of North Slope Farm near Lambertville, New Jersey. Mike has since passed the seed on to Great Road Farm. I'm proud to carry on the tradition, and every year I replant this gigantic, sweet paste tomato, then save the seeds for the following season. Seeds need to be shared and passed along from one generation to the next—traditions like this create community, tying you to a place and purpose.

Our 112-acre farm in Skillman, New Jersey, produces terrific salads. If possible, use a variety of baby lettuces, such as Little Gem, Red Oak, Greek Oak and Lollo Rossa. Pouring the dressing down the side of the bowl and gently coating the greens by hand protects the delicate leaves from getting overdressed and going limp.

Place the lettuces in a large bowl of cold water and gently agitate the leaves to remove any dirt, taking care not to bruise the lettuce. Drain on paper towels and pat dry.

Cut the peel and pith from the oranges with a sharp paring knife. Cut the segments free from the membranes, letting them drop into a small bowl.

Whisk together the shallots, vinegar, honey and mustard in a small bowl. Season to taste with salt and pepper. Gradually whisk in the olive oil and continue to whisk until fully emulsified. Taste and adjust the seasoning.

Place the lettuce in a large bowl and spoon the dressing down the side of the bowl. Sprinkle with salt and pepper. With one hand, gently mix the lettuce into the dressing to coat.

To serve, divide the lettuce, oranges and persimmons among 4 chilled plates, then sprinkle with the pomegranate seeds and almonds.

BABY LETTUCE WITH PERSIMMON AND POMEGRANATE

SERVES 4

2 to 4 heads baby lettuce (depending on their size), preferably a mix of varieties
1 orange
1 tablespoon minced shallot
1 tablespoon balsamic vinegar
1½ teaspoons honey
1½ teaspoons Dijon mustard
Kosher salt and freshly ground black pepper
4 tablespoons extra-virgin olive oil
1 Fuyu persimmon, peeled and cut into eighths
Seeds of 1 pomegranate
¼ cup sliced almonds, lightly toasted

CRISPY PIG EAR SALAD WITH MEYER LEMON–CAPER VINAIGRETTE

SERVES 4

FOR THE MEYER LEMON–CAPER VINAIGRETTE:

¼ cup freshly squeezed Meyer lemon juice

1 shallot, minced

2 tablespoons Dijon mustard

2 tablespoons capers, rinsed and finely chopped

½ teaspoon sugar

¼ cup extra-virgin olive oil

Kosher salt and freshly ground black pepper

FOR THE SALAD:

2 large or 4 small pig ears (about 1 pound total)

1 onion, chopped

2 carrots, chopped

2 celery ribs, chopped

1 cup dry white wine

2 fresh thyme sprigs

2 flat-leaf parsley sprigs

2 marjoram sprigs

½ cup all-purpose flour

½ cup cornstarch

Canola oil, for frying

Kosher salt

2 white endives, leaves separated

1 medium radicchio, torn into bite-sized pieces

1½ cups arugula, preferably wild

2 radishes, preferably French breakfast, thinly sliced

What makes this salad great is that the crisp, salty slivers of pig ear make you crave the lemony dressing . . . and the intense tartness of the dressing makes you want another bite of rich pig's ear . . . and the bitter salad greens taste so good with everything . . . and on and on.

To make the vinaigrette, stir together the lemon juice, shallots, mustard, capers and sugar in a small bowl. Slowly add the oil in a thin stream, whisking constantly to emulsify. Season to taste with salt and pepper. Set aside until ready to use.

Put the pig ears, onions, carrots, celery and wine in a medium pot. Tie the herbs together with some kitchen twine and add to the pot. Add enough water to cover the ears. Bring the pot to a boil, then reduce the heat to low and simmer gently, uncovered, until the ears are very supple and can be easily pierced with a fork, about 2 hours.

Remove the ears from the broth and let cool. Strain the stock through a fine-mesh sieve and reserve for another use.

When cooled, pat the ears dry with paper towels and cut into ¼-inch-thick slivers. Whisk together the flour and cornstarch in a large bowl. Working in batches, add the ears and toss until lightly and uniformly coated with the flour mixture.

Heat at least 3 inches of oil to 350°F in a deep fryer or large saucepan with high sides. Working in batches, gently slip the ears into the hot oil and fry, carefully stirring so they don't stick to each other, until golden brown and crisp, 2 to 3 minutes. Using a slotted spoon, transfer the ears to drain on paper towels and sprinkle with salt.

Combine the endive leaves, radicchio and arugula in a large bowl. Add the radishes and 5 tablespoons of the vinaigrette and gently toss to coat. Taste, adding a little more dressing if needed. Divide the salad between 4 salad plates, top with the crispy pig ears, and serve.

We make this gorgeous salad when the farm is abundant with freshly dug carrots.

Using a vegetable peeler, firmly peel each carrot lengthwise to create long ribbons, rotating the carrot as you work so the ribbons are all the same width. Stop peeling when you reach the core, then discard (or save as a snack). Place the ribbons in a large bowl. Add the radishes, raisins, pine nuts and chives.

Whisk together the olive oil, vinegar, salt and pepper in a small bowl. Pour the vinaigrette over the carrots and toss to coat evenly. To serve, divide the salad among 4 plates and garnish with the sprouts if you like.

CARROT SALAD WITH RADISHES, GOLDEN RAISINS AND PINE NUTS

SERVES 4

5 large carrots, preferably a mixture of yellow, red, purple and orange, peeled
4 radishes, thinly sliced
2 tablespoons golden raisins
2 tablespoons pine nuts, toasted
1 tablespoon minced chives

2 tablespoons extra-virgin olive oil
2 tablespoons rice wine vinegar
¾ teaspoon kosher salt
½ teaspoon freshly ground black pepper
Radish sprouts, for garnish (optional)

FROM THE FARMER
Carrots: A Rainbow of Choices

Carrots are a workhorse of the kitchen—always busy flavoring stocks, soups and sauces. It's easy to forget that their stunning sweetness deserves a starring role from time to time. In addition to the familiar orange varieties, we grow purple, yellow, white and red carrots throughout the season at the farm. Used together on the plate, they can turn a simple carrot salad into a rainbow of color and crunch. Roasted, their sweetness intensifies.

Carrots thrive in loose, deep, well-watered soil. We plant in permanent raised beds that are worked with a broad fork and a walk-behind tractor, which helps limit soil compaction. We harvest carrots by hand with a digging fork, carefully pulling each carrot out with respect and even a little awe. Harvesting some carrots early gives us true baby carrots that are favorites of children at the farmer's market and adults at the restaurant. Carrots harvested after a frost become sugary sweet, better than any candy.

ROASTED BEET AND SPICY CARROT SALAD WITH YOGURT

SERVES 4

6 medium red or golden beets
6 fresh thyme sprigs plus
    1 teaspoon fresh thyme
    leaves
½ cup extra-virgin olive oil
Kosher salt and freshly ground
    black pepper
2 tablespoons red wine vinegar
1 tablespoon freshly squeezed
    lemon juice

8 baby carrots, peeled
1 garlic clove, chopped
½ teaspoon cumin seeds
¼ teaspoon dried red chili
    flakes
1 orange
1 lemon
½ cup whole milk yogurt
¼ cup sunflower seeds, toasted
1 tablespoon chopped chives

Although we think of this colorful, warm salad as a first course, it can make a satisfying vegetarian supper all on its own. Serve it with toasted pita bread, or bake some Flatbread Dough (page 64), seasoned simply with salt and pepper and a drizzle of good olive oil. We make our own yogurt for this dish, but a good-quality organic whole milk yogurt works just fine.

Preheat the oven to 400°F. Put the beets and thyme sprigs on a large piece of aluminum foil. Drizzle with 1 tablespoon olive oil and season with salt and pepper. Wrap tightly with the foil and roast until the beets are tender, 45 minutes to 1 hour. Reduce the oven temperature to 350°F.

Let the beets cool slightly, then peel and cut into wedges. Place in a bowl, and season with salt and pepper. Add 1 tablespoon vinegar, lemon juice and 1 tablespoon olive oil. Toss gently to combine.

Cook the carrots in a pot of boiling salted water until tender (a knife pierces them easily), about 20 minutes. Drain well.

Meanwhile, using a mortar and pestle, pound the garlic, cumin seeds, chili flakes and thyme leaves until crushed and pasty. Season to taste with salt and pepper. Add the remaining 1 tablespoon vinegar and the remaining 6 tablespoons olive oil and continue pounding until well mixed. (Alternatively, pulse the mixture in a blender or food processor.)

Arrange the carrots in a single layer in a medium roasting pan. Spoon the spice mixture over the carrots then squeeze the juice from the orange and lemon over the carrots. Roast until the carrots are golden brown, about 25 minutes. Transfer the carrots to a platter and let cool to room temperature.

To serve, make a pool of yogurt on 4 plates and arrange the beets and carrots on top. Garnish with the toasted sunflower seeds and chopped chives.

It's always fun to create dishes that play on a theme, showing off a single ingredient or idea in several ways. This salad of celery root, celery and celery leaves, plus apples and an apple cider vinaigrette, is a perfect example of how much variety you can tease out of a few ingredients.

Preheat the oven to 350°F. Line a baking sheet with a silicone baking mat or a piece of parchment paper.

Put the brown sugar in a mixing bowl and add hot water, stirring with a rubber spatula, until the sugar has the consistency of very wet sand. Add the walnuts and toss to coat completely. Arrange the sugared walnuts in a single layer on the baking sheet and bake for 5 minutes. Stir the nuts with the spatula and continue to bake, stirring every 3 to 5 minutes, until the nuts look dry to the touch, about 10 minutes more. Remove from the oven and transfer the nuts to a bowl. When cool enough to handle, use your fingers to break the walnuts up into smaller pieces. Set aside.

Whisk together the olive oil, vinegar, ½ teaspoon kosher salt and ¼ teaspoon pepper in a small bowl. Add the raisins and set aside.

Cut the celery root into thin matchsticks and place in a large bowl. Discard the thick outer ribs from the celery heart (save them for another use, such as making stock). Thinly slice the tender, pale green inner celery ribs on the bias; you should have about 1 cup. Add to the celery root. Core the apple and cut it into thin matchsticks; add to the celery root, along with the vinaigrette. Toss well to coat, then let the salad sit until slightly wilted, about 10 minutes. Taste and adjust the seasonings. Add the celery leaves, parsley leaves and candied walnuts, toss again, and serve.

CELERY ROOT SALAD WITH APPLES AND WALNUTS

SERVES 4 TO 6

½ cup packed light brown sugar
3 to 4 teaspoons hot water
1 cup walnuts
3 tablespoons extra-virgin olive oil
1½ tablespoons apple cider vinegar
Kosher salt and freshly ground black pepper
⅓ cup golden raisins
1 large celery root (about 1½ pounds), trimmed and peeled
1 celery heart
1 apple
½ cup celery leaves
¼ cup flat-leaf Italian parsley leaves

Described as a "perfect salad" by Fran Schumer of The New York Times, this is the most requested first course on Agricola's menu. It was the brain-child of our chef de cuisine Manlee Siu. One of the best things about this recipe is that it's not written in stone. During the fall and winter, we make this version with its roasted cauliflower and cubes of sweet-tart pickled pumpkin, but in other months we've garnished the salad with pickled mushrooms, fresh and pickled radishes, carrots, rainbow chard stems...the sky's the limit, so have fun!

Put the cilantro, ¼ cup pumpkin seeds, the roasted garlic, lime juice, maple syrup, brown sugar, ginger and salt in a blender and blend until very smooth. While the motor is running, add the oil in a slow stream and blend until emulsified. Transfer the dressing to a bowl and refrigerate until ready to use.

To serve, put the kale and 1 cup of the dressing into a large bowl and, with clean hands, firmly squeeze the dressing and kale together until the leaves break down and the volume has been reduced by about half. Divide the dressed kale between 4 plates or bowls and garnish with the roasted cauliflower, pickled pump-kin and the remaining ¼ cup toasted pumpkin seeds.

THE FAMOUS KALE SALAD

SERVES 4 TO 6

2 cups lightly packed cilantro leaves
½ cup pumpkin seeds, toasted
2 roasted garlic cloves, peeled
2 tablespoons freshly squeezed lime juice
2 tablespoons maple syrup
1 tablespoon brown sugar
1 teaspoon finely grated fresh ginger
½ teaspoon kosher salt
½ cup grapeseed oil
16 curly kale leaves (from about 2 bunches), ribs discarded and leaves torn into bite-sized pieces
2 cups Roasted Cauliflower (page 142)
1½ cups Pickled Pumpkin (page 179)

Kale: Hearty, Healthful, Spectacular

Overwintered kale was the first crop we shipped to Agricola. We had planted it at the end of summer so that it could go into a hibernation of sorts over the winter. Come spring, longer days and warmer weather send a signal to the kale—it's time to produce flowers that then form seeds to complete the plant's life cycle. Because it has converted its sugars during the winter's freezing temperatures, overwintered kale has especially tender, sweet leaves and its pretty flowers are edible. This all helps produce a spectacular Kale Salad (page 53), and is well worth the hard work needed to harvest it. Flowering kale produces small bushy leaves that need to be handpicked individually. It may take 50 to 75 small leaves to make 1 pound. (To compare, later in the season, it will only take about 20 large leaves of kale to equal a pound.)

While flowering kale is a special treat we look forward to every spring, we grow Red Russian, Blue Curled Scottish (a.k.a. curly) and Toscano kales throughout the year. We are thrilled that this hearty, healthful green has worked its way into the public's consciousness, and that it's so easy to grow in our climate.

Josh drew from his Jewish background for this delicious potato salad topped with big flakes of smoked whitefish. It was a huge hit on Agricola's first Thanksgiving menu. We get our whitefish from Acme Smoked Fish, which has been smoking fish in Brooklyn since 1906. This recipe will make more mustard vinaigrette than you need for the salad; hold on to it for smearing on a roast beef or ham sandwich.

To make the mustard vinaigrette, put the lemon juice, vinegar, mustard, garlic and egg yolk in a bowl and whisk together until well combined. Whisking constantly, slowly add the oil in a thin stream, and whisk until thickened and creamy. Season with salt and pepper. Refrigerate until ready to use.

Put the potatoes in a pot with the thyme and 2 tablespoons salt. Cover the potatoes with cold water, then bring to a boil. Reduce the heat to moderately low and simmer until tender, 15 to 20 minutes. Drain the potatoes and discard the thyme sprigs. When cool enough to handle, slice the potatoes into ¼-inch-thick rounds and place in a bowl.

Prepare an ice water bath. Blanch the carrots and celery in a small pot of boiling salted water until tender, about 2 minutes. Drain the vegetables and add to the ice water to cool completely. Drain well and pat dry with paper towels.

Add the carrots, celery and shallots to the potatoes. Add ¼ to ⅓ cup of the mustard vinaigrette and gently stir to combine, adding a little water to loosen the dressing if needed. Season with salt and pepper then gently fold in the parsley and chives.

Peel the skin off the whitefish. Carefully pull the 2 filets from the center bone, keeping the flesh intact. Gently run your fingers down the flesh and, with tweezers, pull out any pin bones. Break the fish into generous chunks.

To serve, divide the potato salad among 4 plates and top with the chunks of fish. Garnish with radish sprouts, if you like.

SMOKED WHITEFISH AND FINGERLING POTATO SALAD

SERVES 4

3 tablespoons freshly squeezed lemon juice
2 tablespoons champagne vinegar
1 tablespoon Dijon mustard
1 garlic clove, minced
1 large egg yolk
½ cup extra-virgin olive oil
Kosher salt and freshly ground black pepper
1½ pounds small fingerling potatoes

4 fresh thyme sprigs
1 large carrot, finely diced
1 large celery rib, finely diced
3 shallots, minced
1 tablespoon chopped flat-leaf parsley leaves
1 tablespoon minced chives
1 pound whole smoked whitefish
Handful of radish sprouts, for garnish (optional)

FLATBREADS

A CRISPY, CHEWY CRUST

MUSHROOM, SPINACH AND CRACKED EGG FLATBREAD

SERVES 4

FOR THE GARLIC OIL:
½ cup extra-virgin olive oil
6 garlic cloves, peeled

FOR THE FLATBREAD:
1 recipe Flatbread Dough,
    divided into 4 balls
    (page 64)
¾ cup fresh ricotta cheese
4 cups sliced assorted
    mushrooms, such as
    shiitake and oyster
3 cups baby spinach leaves
2 tablespoons fresh oregano
    leaves, chopped
Dried red chili flakes, to taste
Kosher salt and freshly ground
    black pepper
4 large eggs
¼ cup freshly grated
    Parmigiano Reggiano

This flatbread appeared on our opening night's menu and has been so popular that we've never taken it off. It showcases Great Road Farm's delicious brown eggs, as well as the beautiful mushrooms from nearby Shibumi Farm.

To make the garlic oil, heat the olive oil and garlic in a small saucepan over moderately low heat until simmering. Reduce the heat to low and cook gently until the garlic is lightly browned, about 10 minutes. Remove from the heat and let cool. Strain the cooled oil through a fine-mesh sieve; discard the garlic.

Place a pizza stone in the oven and preheat the oven to 500°F.

Roll or stretch 1 portion of dough out onto a lightly floured pizza peel into any shape you like—round, square or the rectangular shape we serve at the restaurant. Spread 3 tablespoons ricotta over the dough, leaving a ½-inch border around the edge.

Combine the mushrooms, spinach, oregano and chili flakes in a large bowl. Season to taste with salt and pepper. Spread a quarter of the mushroom mixture over the ricotta.

Drizzle with some of the garlic oil.

Slide the flatbread onto the hot pizza stone and bake for 5 minutes. Open the oven and carefully crack 1 of the eggs over the center of the flatbread. Continue to bake until the crust is golden brown and the egg yolk is still runny, about 5 minutes more. Transfer the flatbread to a cutting board and sprinkle 1 tablespoon Parmesan over it. Cut into pieces and serve at once. Repeat with the remaining balls of dough and toppings.

DUCK CONFIT FLATBREAD WITH TURNIPS, GOAT CHEESE AND CARAMELIZED ONION

SERVES 4

4 tablespoons cold unsalted
butter
1 sweet onion (about
8 ounces), chopped
Kosher salt
1 pound white turnips, peeled
and roughly chopped
2 cups Vegetable Stock (page
194)
1 recipe Flatbread Dough,
divided into 4 balls
(page 64)

3 cups coarsely shredded Duck
Confit Legs (page 102)
1 cup caramelized yellow
onions
2 cups crumbled goat cheese
2 tablespoons fresh thyme
leaves, chopped
Garlic Oil (page 60)
4 tablespoons freshly grated
Parmigiano Reggiano

Inspired by a classic soubise sauce made of onions, rice and cream, we tinkered with the idea, replacing the rice and dairy with sweet, tender turnips. The silky sauce makes a beautiful canvas for a tangle of duck confit, caramelized onions and goat cheese.

Melt 2 tablespoons butter in a sauté pan over low heat. Add the sweet onions and season with salt. Cover the pan and cook, stirring occasionally, until softened, 20 to 25 minutes. Uncover and continue to cook just until most of the liquid has evaporated.

Add the turnips and enough stock to just cover the vegetables. Increase the heat and bring to a boil then decrease the heat to moderately low and simmer until the turnips are soft, about 30 minutes, adding more stock if needed.

Cut the remaining 2 tablespoons cold butter into small pieces. Transfer the turnip mixture to a blender and blend until smooth (use caution when blending hot liquids). With the blender running, gradually add the pieces of cold butter and blend until silky smooth. Set aside.

Place a baking stone in the oven and preheat to 500°F.

Roll or stretch 1 portion of dough out onto a lightly floured pizza peel into any shape you prefer—circle, square or the rectangular shape we serve at the restaurant.

Spread 3 tablespoons of the turnip purée over the dough, leaving a ½-inch border around the edge. Sprinkle ¾ cup of the duck confit, ¼ cup caramelized onions and ½ cup crumbled goat cheese over the purée. Garnish with thyme leaves and drizzle some of the garlic oil over everything. Slide the flatbread into the oven onto the hot stone and bake until the dough is golden brown and crisp, 8 to 10 minutes.

Transfer the flatbread to a cutting board and garnish with some of the freshly grated Parmigiano Reggiano. Cut into pieces and serve immediately. Repeat with the remaining balls of dough and toppings.

Turnips: Sweet and Full of Flavor

Too many people only know turnips as a vegetable that's usually boiled to death. How sad! There's a wide variety of salad turnips that are crisp, juicy and beguilingly sweet. Hakurei, White Egg and Des Vertus Marteau, a French heirloom variety, are just a few of these sweet salad turnips. In the spring, we direct-seed them very close together in our permanent raised beds. They only take about 30 days to reach full size, and as they grow, we make sure they remain weeded and watered. Since they are seeded so close together the young plants compete for space and nutrients. This allows us to thin by harvesting: We pull the smaller turnips, which are great to garnish a dish, to provide space for the other turnips to grow to full size. We extend the season into early winter by growing storage turnips, like the Purple Top, Gold Ball and Gilfeather. These are best used for cooking, as they are larger and firmer then salad turnips. Cooked well, they will be mellow and creamy, a terrific alternative to potatoes.

FLATBREAD DOUGH

This dough should be quite soft, which results in a wonderfully crisp and chewy crust. It freezes well, and it's worth making extra so you'll be ready the next time you have a flatbread craving.

MAKES ABOUT 1¼ POUNDS DOUGH,
ENOUGH FOR 4 FLATBREADS

2 teaspoons dry yeast
¾ cup lukewarm water plus
   1 cup cold water
⅔ cup bread flour
3 to 4 cups unbleached
   all-purpose flour

1 teaspoon kosher salt
1 tablespoon extra-virgin olive
   oil, plus more for oiling
   the bowl

To make the sponge, dissolve the yeast in ¾ cup lukewarm water. Stir in the bread flour. Let the sponge mixture sit, covered with a clean dish towel, until bubbly, about 30 minutes.

Mix together 3 cups all-purpose flour and salt in another bowl. Measure out 1 cup of the flour mixture and stir it into the sponge along with 1 cup cold water. Mix thoroughly and let sit, covered with the dish towel, for another 30 minutes.

Add the olive oil and the remaining flour mixture and knead, by hand or using an electric mixer with a dough hook, until soft and elastic, about 5 minutes. You may have to add a little more flour if the dough is very sticky.

Put the dough in a large, well-oiled bowl, cover with plastic wrap, and let rise at room temperature until doubled in size, about 2 hours. (At the restaurant, we let the dough rise overnight in the refrigerator, which is both convenient and gives the dough more flavor.) Punch the dough down and divide into 4 equal portions, forming each portion into a smooth ball. Arrange the dough balls on an oiled baking sheet, cover with plastic wrap, and let rest at room temperature until ready to use.

Shibumi Farm Mushrooms

Alan Kaufman doesn't just grow the most flavorful shiitake, maitake and portobello mushrooms. He is also a visionary and an educator, preaching the power of mushrooms to improve personal and environmental health.

After twenty-five years as an investment manager, Alan found he had little passion left for the business. In 2003, he began growing mushrooms as a hobby, which led to a broader interest in alternative agricultural methods and to consulting assignments in third world countries. "I was struck by the challenges farmers faced in these areas, but equally by their resourcefulness," Alan says.

In 2010, he became involved with a program in Vietnam called "Mushrooms with a Mission," which aimed to improve the livelihoods and reduce the poverty of 1,000 survivors of landmine accidents and their families in Quang Tri province, while funding removal of unexploded bombs. Many of the farming families in this program are disabled, female-headed households. "Mushrooms are a high value product all over the world and the growing is not land-intensive or physically demanding." Alan explains. "So, even on a small scale, mushroom farming was able to make a meaningful impact on these families and their communities' health and welfare."

After that trip to Vietnam, Alan and his wife took the plunge into farming mushrooms full time. They started in their garage but have since expanded a large, hangar-like space that enables Alan to grow many varieties of mushrooms at a time, each in their own climate-controlled room. He raises saprophytic mushrooms, or "primary decomposers" that help decompose fallen trees, grass clippings, compost or leaf piles, and return to the environment. White button, cremini and portobello mushrooms are the most common saprophytic varieties, as well as shiitakes, maitakes (aka hen of the woods), trumpet and oyster mushrooms, many of which appear regularly on Agricola's menu.

In August, when New Jersey sweet corn is abundant, we want to eat it every day, on everything, including this savory, satisfying flatbread.

Place a pizza stone in the oven and preheat the oven to 500°F.

Prepare a small ice water bath. Cut off the dark green parts of the leeks and discard. Cut the white and light green parts of the leeks into ½-inch rounds. Put the leeks into a bowl of lukewarm water and gently swish to separate the rounds and to remove any dirt. Carefully lift the leeks out of the water, leaving any sediment in the bottom of the bowl. Repeat if necessary.

Cook the leeks in a small pot of salted boiling water for 5 minutes, then drain and transfer to the ice water bath. When completely cooled, transfer to paper towels to drain.

Heat the vegetable stock and butter in a large sauté pan over moderate heat. When the stock begins to simmer, add the leeks and cook until the liquid has reduced enough to just coat the leeks. Remove from the heat and season to taste with salt and pepper. Set aside.

Cook the bacon in a medium sauté pan over moderate heat, stirring occasionally, until crisp, 8 to 10 minutes. Using a slotted spoon, transfer the bacon to paper towels to drain.

Put the kale, olive oil and lemon juice in a large bowl and toss well to combine. Add the corn kernels, bacon and leeks to the kale and season with salt and pepper.

Roll or stretch 1 portion of dough out onto a lightly floured pizza peel into any shape you prefer—round, square or the rectangular shape we serve at the restaurant. Spread 3 tablespoons ricotta over the dough, leaving a ½-inch border around edge. Spread a quarter of the vegetable mixture over the dough and drizzle with some of the garlic oil.

Slide the flatbread onto the hot pizza stone and bake until the crust is golden brown, 8 to 10 minutes. Transfer the flatbread to a cutting board and sprinkle with some of the Parmigiano Reggiano. Cut into pieces and serve at once. Repeat with the remaining balls of dough and toppings.

CORN, BACON AND KALE FLATBREAD

SERVES 4

2 leeks
3 tablespoons Vegetable Stock (page 194) or water
1 tablespoon unsalted butter, unsalted
Kosher salt and freshly ground black pepper
6 ounces smoked bacon, diced
1 cup thinly sliced curly kale
1 tablespoon extra-virgin olive oil

1 teaspoon freshly squeezed lemon juice
1 cup fresh corn kernels
1 recipe Flatbread Dough, divided into 4 balls (page 64)
¾ cup fresh ricotta cheese
Garlic Oil (page 60)
2 tablespoons finely grated Parmigiano Reggiano

HEIRLOOM TOMATO FLATBREAD WITH MOZZARELLA AND BASIL

SERVES 4

1 recipe Flatbread Dough, divided into 4 balls (page 64)

4 tablespoons extra-virgin olive oil

4 pounds ripe heirloom tomatoes, preferably a variety of different kinds and sizes, sliced

2 pounds Fresh Mozzarella (page 118)

2 tablespoons fresh thyme leaves, chopped

Kosher salt and freshly ground black pepper

4 tablespoons finely grated Parmigiano Reggiano

Large handful of fresh basil leaves, torn

Nothing beats a ripe Jersey tomato, and we are always thinking about different ways to serve them. Loaded with heirloom tomatoes and our housemade mozzarella, this is the Agricola spin on a classic New Jersey "tomato pie."

Place a baking stone in the oven and preheat to 500°F.

Roll or stretch 1 portion of dough out onto a lightly floured pizza peel into any shape you prefer—circle, square or the rectangular shape we serve at the restaurant.

Spread 1 tablespoon olive oil over the dough, leaving a ½-inch border around the edge. Arrange a quarter of the tomato slices evenly over the dough. Take a quarter of the mozzarella and tear off small pieces, sprinkling them around and over the tomatoes. Garnish with some of the thyme leaves and season with salt and pepper.

Slide the flatbread into the oven onto the hot stone and bake until the crust is golden brown and crisp, 8 to 10 minutes.

Transfer the flatbread to a cutting board and garnish with some of the freshly grated Parmigiano Reggiano and the torn basil leaves. Cut into pieces and serve immediately. Repeat with the remaining balls of dough and toppings.

FISH &
SEAFOOD

FROM NEARBY WATERS

TILEFISH WITH GNOCCHI AND BLACK TRUMPET FRICASSEE

SERVES 4

FOR THE GNOCCHI:

4 medium russet potatoes

About 2½ cups all-purpose
    flour

3 large eggs

½ cup (1 stick) unsalted butter,
    melted

3 tablespoons finely grated
    Parmigiano Reggiano

1 tablespoon chopped chives

Kosher salt and freshly grated
    black pepper

FOR THE FRICASSEE:

4 parsnips, peeled and chopped
    into ½-inch pieces

4 tablespoons extra-virgin
    olive oil

Kosher salt and freshly ground
    black pepper

1 cup shelled fresh sweet peas

8 ounces smoked bacon, diced

6 baby leeks, sliced

4 tablespoons unsalted butter

6 fresh thyme sprigs

8 ounces black trumpet
    mushrooms, trimmed and
    sliced

½ cup Vegetable Stock
    (page 194)

FOR THE TILEFISH:

Four 6-ounce golden tilefish
    filets, skin on, about
    1¼-inch thick

Kosher salt and freshly ground
    black pepper

1 tablespoon unsalted butter

1 tablespoon canola oil

The coast of New Jersey has some of the best fishing grounds for tilefish in the Northeast. The farther out and the deeper you drop your line, the better the catch. Along the continental shelf, golden tilefish feast on red crabs, which impart a sweet, delicate flavor, similar to that of lobster. For the fricassee, cooking all the vegetables separately and then combining them at the last minute helps to preserve their individual colors, flavors and textures. The gnocchi with fricassee makes a lovely small meal by itself, as does the tilefish with fricassee.

To make the gnocchi, preheat the oven to 400°F. Pierce the potatoes in several places with a fork and bake until soft, about 1 hour. Peel the potatoes and mash the hot flesh through a ricer into a bowl. Set aside the potatoes to cool.

Put the flour in a large bowl and form a well in the center of it. Crack the eggs into the well and stir with your fingertips or a fork, gradually mixing in some of the flour. Add the mashed potatoes and stir to incorporate, mixing in more of the flour. Add the melted butter, Parmesan and chopped chives and stir until the mixture is evenly moistened and shaggy-looking. Season to taste with salt and pepper.

Turn the mixture out onto a lightly floured work surface and knead until the dough comes together and is smooth, sprinkling lightly with flour if it is very sticky. Divide the dough into 6 pieces. Roll each piece between your hands and the work surface into a ¾-inch-thick rope. Cut each rope into ¾-inch pieces.

Prepare an ice water bath. Working in batches, cook the gnocchi in a large pot of boiling salted water until they rise to the surface. Continue to simmer the gnocchi, stirring occasionally, until cooked through and tender, about 45 seconds after they rise to the surface. Using a slotted spoon, transfer the gnocchi to the ice water bath and let cool completely. Drain carefully and spread out on a paper towel while you prepare the rest of the dish. (The gnocchi can be cooked up to 1 day ahead and refrigerated.)

To make the fricassee, preheat the oven to 400°F. Toss the parsnips with 2 tablespoons olive oil and season with salt and pepper. Spread the parsnips out on a baking sheet and roast in the oven until golden brown, about 30 minutes. (Note that a little browning makes parsnips sweeter, but they will become bitter if they get too dark.) Remove from the heat and transfer to a plate.

Meanwhile, prepare a small ice water bath. Cook the peas in a medium pot of salted boiling water until bright green, about 1 minute. Drain the peas, transfer to the ice water bath and cool completely. Drain the peas well and set aside.

Cook the diced bacon in a medium sauté pan over moderate heat, stirring occasionally, until browned and crisp, 8 to 10 minutes. Remove from the heat and transfer to a paper towel–lined plate to drain and cool.

Heat 1 tablespoon olive oil in the cleaned sauté pan over moderately low heat. Add the leeks, season with salt and pepper and cook, stirring occasionally, until tender, about 5 minutes. Add 1 tablespoon butter and 3 thyme sprigs and cook, stirring occasionally, for 5 minutes more. Remove from the heat, discard the thyme and transfer to a plate.

Heat a large sauté pan over moderate heat. Add 1 tablespoon olive oil, and then add the mushrooms. Season with salt and pepper. Cook without stirring until they begin to brown, about 3 minutes. Stir, then add 1 tablespoon butter and the remaining thyme. Cook until the mushrooms are browned and tender, 5 to 7 minutes more. Remove from the heat and transfer to a plate.

To make the tilefish, preheat the oven to 350°F. Season the filets with salt and pepper. Heat the butter and canola oil in a large, heavy sauté pan over moderately high heat. Add the fish and cook until browned on each side, about 6 minutes total. Transfer the pan to the oven and roast until the fish is opaque and cooked through, about 7 minutes.

To finish the fricassee, heat a large sauté pan over moderately high heat. Add the remaining 2 tablespoons butter. When the butter foams, add the gnocchi and 3 tablespoons vegetable stock. Add the reserved bacon, mushrooms, leeks, parsnips and peas and cook, stirring gently, until heated through, about 5 minutes, adding a little more vegetable stock if needed to loosen the fricassee. Season to taste with salt and pepper.

To serve, divide the gnocchi and mushroom fricassee among 4 warm plates and top with the roasted tilefish.

Ask your fishmonger to "pan-dress" the fish, which means removing the head, dorsal fin and gill plate, but leaving the tail. This allows you to open the trout flat, like a book, which makes it easy to cook (and to eat). Plan to make the vinaigrette ahead and rewarm it gently at serving time. The garnish of sliced almonds is traditional with trout, but feels new in this summery dish.

Bring a large pot of water to a boil and generously season with salt. Prepare an ice water bath. Put the tomatoes in a sieve and dip in the boiling water for 30 seconds, then dip in the ice water bath until cooled. Drain the tomatoes well, and pull off and discard their skins. Set the tomatoes aside.

Add the string beans to the boiling water and cook until just tender, 4 to 5 minutes. Transfer to the ice water bath. Drain the cooled beans and pat dry with paper towels.

To make the vinaigrette, cut half of the peeled cherry tomatoes in half. Heat 2 tablespoons olive oil in a medium saucepan over moderate heat. Add the shallots and cook, stirring often, until softened, about 1 minute. Add all of the tomatoes and cook, stirring occasionally, until they begin to release their juices, 4 to 6 minutes. Remove from the heat and stir in the vinegar and 2 tablespoons olive oil. Season to taste with salt and pepper. Set aside.

Season the trout on both sides with salt and pepper. Heat 2 large sauté pans over medium-high heat (the fish are large when opened; if you only have 1 pan, you will have to cook them in 2 batches). Add 1 tablespoon olive oil to each pan and swirl to coat the pan. Add the trout, skin side down, and cook for 2 to 3 minutes. Flip carefully and cook for another 2 minutes. Remove from the pan and transfer to a warm platter. Cover loosely to keep warm.

Wipe out one of the sauté pans and heat the remaining 2 tablespoons olive oil over moderately high heat. Add the beans and cook briefly, just until warmed through. Season to taste with salt and pepper. Meanwhile, gently reheat the vinaigrette.

To serve, place each trout, skin side down, on the center of a warm plate. Top each fish with a quarter of the beans. Spoon the warm tomato vinaigrette over the beans and garnish with the toasted almonds.

RAINBOW TROUT WITH CHERRY TOMATO VINAIGRETTE AND SUMMER BEANS

SERVES 4

1 pint cherry tomatoes
8 ounces string beans, preferably a mix of yellow wax and green beans, trimmed
½ cup extra-virgin olive oil
1 large shallot, minced
1 tablespoon red wine vinegar
Kosher salt and freshly ground black pepper
Four 10-ounce whole rainbow trout, boned and pan-dressed
¾ cup sliced almonds, lightly toasted

MONKFISH WITH LENTILS, ROASTED MIREPOIX AND GREMOLATA

SERVES 4

9 tablespoons extra-virgin olive oil,

3 tablespoons finely chopped yellow onion

1 cup dried green lentils, preferably French green lentils ("lentilles du Puy")

2 cups Vegetable Stock (page 194)

Kosher salt and freshly ground black pepper

3 large carrots, diced

3 large celery ribs, diced

1 medium red onion, diced

3 tablespoons finely chopped flat-leaf parsley leaves

1 teaspoon finely grated lemon zest

2 garlic cloves, minced

1½ pounds monkfish, cut into 4 pieces

Monkfish may be recognized for its huge, ugly head and toothy mouth, but the tail is the only edible part of the fish. The dense white flesh is often tagged "poor man's lobster" because of its mild sweetness and meaty texture. Whether you get monkfish whole or filleted, you will have to remove the tough silvery membrane that surrounds the meat. Then, because of its long tapering shape, it's best to portion out the tail so that it cooks evenly.

To make the lentils, heat 1 tablespoon olive oil in a saucepan over moderate heat. Add the yellow onions and cook until softened and translucent, about 5 minutes. Add the lentils and vegetable stock. Bring to a boil, then reduce the heat and simmer until the lentils are tender, 20 to 25 minutes. Drain the lentils in a colander then transfer to a bowl, drizzle with 1 tablespoon olive oil and season with salt and pepper. Cover loosely to keep warm.

To make the mirepoix, preheat the oven to 425°F. Toss the carrots with 2 tablespoons olive oil and season with salt and pepper. Spread the carrots out on a baking sheet and roast, stirring once, until tender and caramelized, 12 to 15 minutes. Toss the celery and red onion with 2 tablespoons olive oil and season with salt and pepper. Spread out on another baking sheet and roast, stirring once, until tender and caramelized, about 10 minutes. Gently toss all the vegetables together and cover loosely to keep warm.

While the vegetables roast, make the gremolata. Stir together the parsley, lemon zest and garlic in a small bowl. Set aside.

Season the fish with salt and pepper. Heat 3 tablespoons olive oil in a large sauté pan over moderately high heat. Add the fish and cook until the underside is browned, 3 to 4 minutes. Rotate the fish a quarter turn and cook for 2 minutes. Continue to turn and cook until browned all over, 8 to 10 minutes total.

To serve, spoon the warm lentils onto 4 plates. Place the vegetables on one side of the lentils and the monkfish on the other side. Garnish the fish with a sprinkling of gremolata.

A member of the ray family, skate has two triangular side fins that resemble wings. These wings, the edible portions of skate, are divided by cartilage rather than bones and, once cleaned, have a striated appearance. The meat is creamy, tender and easy to cook. This recipe makes more pomegranate vinaigrette than you will need—save it and use for salad or to serve over Roasted Cauliflower (page 142).

Bring the parsnips and vegetable stock to a boil in a medium pot, then reduce the heat to moderate, cover, and cook until tender, about 20 minutes.

Using a slotted spoon, transfer the parsnips to a blender, adding about ¾ cup of the cooking liquid, and blend to make a smooth purée. Stir in the butter and season to taste with salt and pepper. Keep warm.

To make the vinaigrette, bring the pomegranate juice to a boil in a medium saucepan over moderately high heat. Reduce the heat to moderate, and cook, stirring occasionally, until reduced to ¼ cup, 15 to 20 minutes. Transfer to a small bowl and cool completely. Whisk in ⅓ cup olive oil, along with the honey, vinegar and mustard. Season to taste with salt and pepper. Set aside.

Put the flour in a shallow bowl. Season the skate wings with salt and pepper, then lightly dredge the wings in the flour, shaking off the excess.

Heat 2 tablespoons olive oil in a large sauté pan over moderately high heat. Add 2 skate wings and cook until golden brown, 2 to 3 minutes. Flip the skate, add 2 thyme sprigs and cook for another 2 minutes. Drain on paper towels. Repeat with the remaining 2 tablespoons olive oil, skate and thyme.

To serve, place a pool of warm parsnip purée on 4 warm plates. Top with the skate and drizzle some of the vinaigrette around the edges of the plates. Garnish the skate with the pomegranate seeds.

PAN-ROASTED SKATE WITH PARSNIP PURÉE AND POMEGRANATE VINAIGRETTE

SERVES 4

4 large parsnips, peeled and chopped
4 cups Vegetable Stock (page 194), or as needed
2 tablespoons unsalted butter
Kosher salt and freshly ground black pepper
1½ cups pomegranate juice
⅓ cup plus ¼ cup extra-virgin olive oil, divided

1 tablespoon plus 2 teaspoons honey
1 teaspoon rice wine vinegar
1 teaspoon Dijon mustard
1 cup flour, preferably Wondra
1½ pounds skate wings, cut into four 6-ounce portions
4 fresh thyme sprigs
¼ cup pomegranate seeds

CAPE MAY SEA SCALLOPS WITH CAULIFLOWER AND CAPER-RAISIN RELISH

SERVES 4

½ cup golden raisins

2 tablespoons Madeira

2 tablespoons capers, rinsed and roughly chopped

¼ cup plus 2½ tablespoons extra-virgin olive oil

2 tablespoons white verjus

1 tablespoon finely chopped flat-leaf parsley leaves

Kosher salt and freshly ground black pepper

1 small head white cauliflower, trimmed and cut into small florets

4 tablespoons unsalted butter, softened

1 head purple, green or yellow cauliflower, cut into small florets

12 large sea scallops

We prepare scallops many different ways throughout the year. In spring, we may serve them with sweet pea purée, morels and ramps, or Black Trumpet Fricassee (page 74). Winter calls for a heartier combination of littleneck clams, mirepoix and black garlic purée. This cauliflower preparation, with its agrodolce flavors and colorful cauliflowers, is a fall favorite. Verjus is the pressed juice of unripe fruit, often white grapes; it offers an acidic tang to sauces but has a gentler flavor than vinegar. Look for it in specialty foods shops. If you can't find colored cauliflower, use more of the white.

To make the relish, stir together the raisins and Madeira in a small bowl and let soak for 20 minutes to plump. Roughly chop the raisins and stir together with the capers, 1½ tablespoons olive oil, verjus and parsley. Season to taste with salt and pepper. Set aside.

To make the cauliflower purée, cook the white cauliflower in a large pot of salted boiling water until tender, about 8 minutes. Drain well. Purée the cauliflower in a food processor until smooth. Add 3 tablespoons of the butter, season with salt and pepper and process for 10 more seconds. Keep warm.

To roast the purple cauliflower, preheat the oven to 400°F. On a large baking sheet, drizzle the cauliflower florets with ¼ cup olive oil. Season with salt and pepper and toss well. Roast, stirring occasionally, until the cauliflower is tender and golden brown, about 30 minutes. Set aside.

For the scallops, heat 1 tablespoon each of the butter and olive oil in a large sauté pan over moderately high heat. If still attached, remove the tough muscle from the side of each scallop and season the scallops on both sides with salt and pepper. When the butter foams, add the scallops and cook until the underside is golden brown, about 2 minutes, then flip and cook for 1 minute more. Remove the scallops from the pan and keep warm.

To serve, make a pool of the cauliflower purée on 4 warm plates. Drag a spoon through the purée, streaking it across the plate. Place 3 scallops on the purée, top each scallop with some of the relish and garnish with the roasted cauliflower.

The French call their seafood stew bouillabaisse; to Italians, it's cioppino. Tomatoes figure prominently in both styles. At Agricola, we do things a little differently, using Great Road Farm turnips, fennel and celery to make a sweet, delicate broth that complements a range of seafood from our mid-Atlantic waters. Shop for the freshest fish you can find, and open a bottle of good chardonnay for the broth, because these ingredients will make a huge difference in the final dish.

Heat half of the oil in a large saucepan over moderately high heat until it is almost smoking. Season the fish and scallops generously with salt and pepper and add half of the seafood to the pan. Sear on all sides, 2 to 3 minutes. Remove the fish and set it aside. Wipe out the pan and repeat with the remaining oil, fish and scallops, setting aside all the seared seafood.

Add the turnips, celery, onions, fennel, potato and garlic to the pan and cook, stirring occasionally, until the vegetables begin to soften, about 2 minutes. Add the clams, wine and bay leaf and bring to a boil. Cover and cook until the clams have opened, 3 to 4 minutes. Using tongs, transfer the clams to a bowl and loosely cover to keep warm (discard any clams that don't open fully). Add the stock and return to a boil. Reduce the heat to moderately low, cover the pan, and simmer for 30 minutes. Remove from the heat and stir in the cream, if using.

Process the soup in a blender until smooth (use caution when blending hot liquids), then transfer to a clean saucepan. Stir in the lemon juice and season to taste with salt. Bring to a simmer over moderate heat.

Add the calamari rings to the soup, along with the seared fish, and cook until all the fish is tender and cooked through, about 8 minutes. Stir in the clams.

To serve, divide the seafood among warmed soup bowls and ladle the soup over the fish. Garnish with the parsley and serve with plenty of warm crusty bread.

EAST COAST SEAFOOD STEW

SERVES 4 TO 6

3 tablespoons extra-virgin olive oil

1½ pounds seafood, such as a combination of monkfish, golden tilefish, snapper, cod and scallops (fish cut into 2-inch pieces)

Kosher salt and freshly ground black pepper

1 pound turnips, peeled and finely chopped

2 celery ribs, finely chopped

1 white onion, finely chopped

1 fennel bulb, cored and finely chopped

1 russet potato, peeled and finely chopped

4 garlic cloves, minced

16 to 20 littleneck clams (about 1 pound), scrubbed

1 cup white wine, such as Chardonnay

1 bay leaf

3 cups Vegetable Stock (page 194)

½ cup heavy cream (optional)

1 tablespoon freshly squeezed lemon juice

½ pound cleaned calamari, cut into rings

1 tablespoon chopped flat-leaf parsley leaves

Crusty bread, for serving

MEAT,
POULTRY
& MORE

HEARTY DISHES & LIGHTER MEALS

OUR "PORK & BEANS"

We like to start this dish with beautiful Berkshire pork chops. Ask your butcher for center cut chops with a generous fat cap. This well-marbled exterior of the pork loin adds flavor to the finished dish. Brining the chops overnight marinates and cures at the same time, producing juicier meat in the end. For the beans, we favor thick-cut bacon, but really, any bacon will do. Before cooking, pop the bacon into the freezer for 10 or 15 minutes; it will be much easier to cut.

SERVES 4

Kosher salt	1 medium yellow onion, diced
3 tablespoons sugar	1 medium ripe tomato, peeled
2 fresh thyme sprigs	and chopped
2 bay leaves	2 garlic cloves, minced
1 teaspoon black peppercorns	⅓ cup maple syrup
2 allspice berries	⅓ cup molasses
1 whole clove	¼ cup dry mustard powder
Four 12-ounce, center cut pork	3 tablespoons cider vinegar
chops, bones frenched	Freshly ground black pepper
1 pound dried navy beans	
8 ounces smoked bacon	

To brine the pork, combine 10 cups cold water, ¼ cup salt, sugar, thyme sprigs, 1 bay leaf, the peppercorns, allspice and clove in a large pot and bring to a boil, stirring to dissolve the salt and sugar. Remove from the heat and let cool.

When the brine has cooled completely, add the pork chops and refrigerate overnight.

Put the beans in a bowl, cover with cold water and soak overnight.

The following day, cut half of the bacon into ½-inch cubes. Cut the other half into 1-inch-thick strips.

Preheat the oven to 300°F. Line the bottom of 4-quart Dutch oven with the onions and cubes of bacon. Drain the beans and pour over the bacon and onions.

Bring 4 cups water to a boil in a saucepan. Add the tomato, garlic, maple syrup, molasses, mustard powder, vinegar, remaining 1 bay leaf, 2 teaspoons salt and 1 teaspoon pepper. Simmer for 1 minute, stir well and pour over the beans. Top the beans with the strips of bacon. Tightly cover the pot and place in the oven. Bake, checking every hour to make sure the liquid is just covering the beans and adding more water if needed, until the beans are fully tender, 4 to 5 hours. When the beans are fully cooked, uncover the pot and continue to bake until the cooking liquid has reduced and thickened, about 30 minutes more. Taste and adjust the seasonings. Keep warm.

About 1 hour before serving, remove the pork chops from the brine, pat dry and bring to room temperature.

Preheat a grill to high. Generously season the pork chops with salt and pepper and drizzle with oil. Grill until the meat near the bone is still pink and an instant-read meat thermometer inserted in the center of the chop registers 145° to 150°F, about 6 minutes per side (12 minutes per inch of thickness). Let the chops rest, loosely covered, for 5 minutes before serving (the temperature will rise a few degrees as they sit).

To serve, spoon some of the beans on 4 warmed plates and top each with a pork chop.

VENISON LOIN WITH BUTTERNUT SQUASH, RED CABBAGE AND BLACKBERRY SAUCE

For years, Josh has used venison from Ed Spoonmaker of Millbrook Venison in New York. Ed's meat is free of chemical additives, and he processes his animals on site. Note that venison is extremely lean and should be cooked no higher than medium rare. When Josh lived on the West Coast, he made this dish with huckleberries, which are abundant in the Pacific Northwest, but East Coasters may find it easier to use blackberries.

SERVES 4

3 pounds venison or beef
   bones
5 tablespoons extra-virgin
   olive oil
1 carrot, chopped
1 celery rib, chopped
1 onion, chopped
1 leek, chopped
6 garlic cloves, chopped
1 tablespoon tomato paste
One 750-ml bottle plus 1 cup
   red wine, preferably
   pinot noir
4 cups Chicken Stock
   (page 195)
10 sprigs fresh thyme
10 juniper berries
10 black peppercorns

2 bay leaves
3 cups blackberries or
   huckleberries
Kosher salt and freshly ground
   black pepper
1 large butternut squash
   (about 1½ pounds), halved
   lengthwise
6 tablespoons unsalted butter
4 cups thinly sliced red
   cabbage
1 tablespoon rice wine vinegar
2 tablespoons sugar
1½ pounds venison loin,
   cut into eight 3-ounce
   medallions
2 tablespoons minced chives

To make the sauce, preheat the oven to 350°F. Place the bones in a roasting pan and roast until golden brown, about 40 minutes.

Heat 2 tablespoons olive oil in a stockpot over moderately high heat. Add the carrots, celery, onions, leeks and garlic and cook, stirring occasionally, until caramelized, about 10 minutes. Add the tomato paste and cook, stirring, about 1 minute. Add the roasted venison bones, red wine, chicken stock, thyme sprigs, juniper berries, peppercorns and bay leaves. Bring to a boil, then reduce the heat and simmer until reduced to about 3 cups, 45 minutes to 1 hour.

Strain the sauce through a fine-mesh sieve into a saucepan. Add 2 cups blackberries and cook over moderate heat until reduced to about 1¼ cups, about 30 minutes. Purée the sauce in a blender, then strain through a fine-mesh sieve back into the cleaned saucepan. Stir in the remaining 1 cup blackberries and season to taste with salt and pepper. Set aside, and keep warm.

To make the squash, preheat the oven to 350°F. Drizzle the squash with 1 tablespoon olive oil then place on a baking sheet, cut side down, and bake until tender, about 45 minutes. Peel and purée the flesh in a food processor with 4 tablespoons butter. Season to taste with salt and pepper.

To make the cabbage, heat the remaining 2 tablespoons butter in a sauté pan over moderate heat. Add the cabbage and cook, stirring occasionally, until wilted, about 5 minutes. Stir in the vinegar, remaining 1 cup wine and sugar and cook, covered, until tender, 25 to 30 minutes. Remove the lid and continue to cook until most of the liquid has been absorbed and the cabbage has turned deep purple, 3 to 4 minutes. Season to taste with salt and pepper. Set aside and keep warm.

To cook the venison, season with salt and pepper. Heat the remaining 2 tablespoons olive oil in a large sauté pan over high heat. Add the medallions and sear until rare to medium rare, about 2 minutes per side.

To serve, make a pool of squash purée on one side of 4 plates and drag the back of a spoon through the purée to streak it across the plate. Place some of the cabbage in the center, top with the venison and drizzle the blackberry sauce around the plate. Garnish with the minced chives. Repeat with remaining plates.

FROM THE FARMER
Winter Squash: Delicata, Acorn and Butternut

At Great Road Farm, around the time of the summer solstice, we plant squash seeds directly in single rows, with the beds spaced about six feet apart. As the plants emerge, this gives us enough room to cultivate between the beds with a tractor to prepare another seed bed that we plant with white clover. The clover acts as a living mulch, fixing nitrogen in the soil and helping to suppress weeds. Eventually our squash fields turn into a wild jungle, with some weeds out-competing the clover and the squash plants sending their runners out, searching for open light and working hard to produce as much fruit as they can.

Around mid-September we begin harvesting the delicata, kabocha and acorn squashes; these varieties are better for fresh eating, while other varieties are good for storage. Butternut is our best keeper, but we always seem to run out of our stored-up supply by December because they are so delicious.

BRAISED BEEF SHORT RIBS

We get our beef short ribs from Creekstone Farms in Arkansas City, Kansas. We find their meat to be consistent and full of flavor, plus their Black Angus cattle are raised without antibiotics or hormones, and are slaughtered as humanely as possible in a facility designed by Temple Grandin.

Before diving into this recipe, note that the ribs need to marinate overnight, and because braises usually taste better when made ahead and reheated, it makes sense to start this recipe a couple of days before you plan to serve it. Serve with puréed potatoes and roasted vegetables—whatever's in season.

SERVES 6 TO 8

One 750-ml bottle red wine, preferably cabernet sauvignon
4 to 4½ pounds boneless beef short ribs, trimmed
1 cup all-purpose flour, for dredging
Kosher salt and freshly ground black pepper
2 tablespoons extra-virgin olive oil
5 garlic cloves, peeled
2 carrots, cut into 1-inch lengths
2 celery ribs, cut into 1-inch lengths
1 leek, white and light green parts only, coarsely chopped
6 flat-leaf parsley sprigs
2 fresh thyme sprigs
2 bay leaves
2 tablespoons tomato paste
2 cups beef demiglace
4 cups Beef Stock (page 195), or as needed

Heat the wine in a large saucepan over moderate heat. When the wine is hot, light a match and carefully set the wine aflame. Let the flames die out, remove from the heat, and cool completely.

Place the short ribs in the cooled wine and marinate, refrigerated, overnight.

Preheat the oven to 350°F. Remove the short ribs from wine and pat dry (reserve the wine). Stir together the flour, 1 tablespoon salt and 1 tablespoon pepper in a shallow bowl. Season the ribs all over with salt and pepper then lightly dredge in the seasoned flour.

Heat the olive oil in a large Dutch oven over moderately high heat. Slip the ribs into the pot and sear until well browned, 3 to 4 minutes per side. Transfer the browned ribs to a plate. Remove all but 1 tablespoon of fat from the pot; lower the heat to moderate, and add the garlic, carrots, celery, leeks, parsley, thyme and bay leaves. Cook, stirring occasionally, until lightly browned, 5 to 7 minutes. Add the tomato paste and cook, stirring constantly, for 1 minute to blend.

Add the demiglace, reserved wine and the ribs to the pot. Add enough stock to almost cover the ribs and bring to a boil. Tightly cover the pot, put it in the oven, and cook until the ribs are tender enough to be easily pierced with a fork, 2½ to 3 hours.

Carefully remove the meat to a platter, cover, and keep warm. Skim off and discard any fat floating on the surface of the cooking liquid. Set the pot over moderate heat and bring the liquid to a boil. Reduce the heat slightly and simmer until the sauce has reduced to about 3 cups, 20 to 25 minutes. Taste periodically to make sure that the sauce is not becoming too salty; if it is, add a little more unsalted beef stock to it. Pour the sauce through a fine-mesh sieve, taste and adjust the seasonings.

To serve, arrange the braised short ribs on a warm platter and pour the sauce over the meat.

BRAISED VEAL SHANK
WITH SALSA VERDE

SERVES 2 TO 3

1 veal shank, about 5 pounds, hock removed

Kosher salt and freshly ground black pepper

3 tablespoons extra-virgin olive oil

2 carrots, chopped

2 celery ribs, chopped

1 leek, chopped

2 garlic cloves, chopped

5 fresh thyme sprigs

2 bay leaves

1 tablespoon dried oregano

1 tablespoon black peppercorns

1 teaspoon fennel seeds

2 cups white wine

2 ripe tomatoes, peeled and chopped

8 cups Beef Stock (page 195)

Salsa Verde (page 32), for serving

Castle Valley Mill Soft Polenta (page 138), for serving

Allow plenty of time when preparing this recipe, because the shank tastes best a day or two after it has been braised. The flavors meld, and the texture of the meat is enhanced by its rest in the braising juices. Served with Salsa Verde and Soft Polenta, it's a dreamy dish for a cold evening.

Preheat the oven to 325°F. Season the veal shank all over with salt and pepper.

Heat the olive oil in a large Dutch oven or deep ovenproof skillet over moderately high heat. Add the veal shank and cook, turning occasionally, until golden brown on all sides, 10 to 15 minutes. Transfer the shank to a plate and add the carrots, celery, leeks, garlic, thyme sprigs, bay leaves, oregano, peppercorns and fennel seeds. Cook, stirring occasionally, until the vegetables are caramelized, 10 to 15 minutes.

Add the wine and tomatoes and deglaze the skillet, using a wooden spoon to stir and scrape the bottom of the pot to loosen the *fond*, or browned bits.

Add the stock, return the veal to the pot (the liquid should come about halfway up the shank), and bring to a simmer. Cover the pot and transfer to the oven. Braise at a very gentle simmer for 2 hours. Remove the lid and skim to remove any floating impurities. If necessary, continue cooking, covered, until a fork can easily pierce the meat, up to 1 hour more. Uncover and let the shank cool in the liquid.

When cool, transfer the shank to a dish and strain the cooking liquid through a fine-mesh sieve into a clean pot. Bring to a simmer and skim again to remove any impurities. Pour the braising liquid over the veal shank. Let cool completely, then cover and refrigerate overnight.

To serve, gently heat the veal shank in its braising liquid. Transfer to a serving platter, spoon some of the braising liquid over the top and garnish with the Salsa Verde. Serve with Soft Polenta on the side.

Flatiron steaks have it all—this economical cut from below the shoulder blade is extremely tender with a big, beefy flavor. To make this meal even heartier, we sometimes top each plate with a poached egg. We love how the yolk spills into the rice and mingles with the spicy kimchi.

Heat a grill over high heat. Season the steaks with salt and pepper and drizzle with the olive oil. Grill the steaks, turning once, until nicely charred, about 5 minutes on each side for medium-rare. Transfer the steaks to a carving board, cover loosely with foil, and let rest for 10 minutes.

While the steaks rest, make the fried rice. Break up the cold rice with your fingers so no clumps remain; set aside. Trim the scallions and separate the white and green parts. Thinly slice the green ends of the scallions and set aside. Thinly slice the white ends and set aside.

Heat the canola oil in a large, deep frying pan or a wok over high heat. Add the sliced scallion whites and cook, stirring constantly, until fragrant and sizzling, about 1 minute. Add the kimchi and chile paste and cook, stirring, until the kimchi begins to soften, 3 to 5 minutes.

Add the cold rice, soy sauce and sesame oil. Mix well so that the rice is coated with the kimchi. (Add a little of the briny liquid from the kimchi if the mixture looks too dry.) Continue cooking, stirring constantly, for just a few more minutes until the rice is warmed through. Add the garlic chives in the last minute of cooking, stir well, and cook just until they start to wilt. Remove from the heat and season with salt to taste.

Slice the steaks thinly against the grain and serve over the rice. Garnish with the reserved scallion greens.

GRILLED FLATIRON STEAKS WITH KIMCHI FRIED RICE

SERVES 4

Four 8-ounce flatiron steaks
Kosher salt and freshly ground black pepper
2 tablespoons extra-virgin olive oil
3 cups cold cooked rice
5 scallions
2 tablespoons canola oil
1 to 1½ cups Napa Cabbage and Daikon Kimchi (page 189), chopped
1 tablespoon *gochujang* (Korean fermented red chile paste)
2 teaspoons light soy sauce
1 teaspoon sesame oil
Kosher salt
½ bunch garlic chives, chopped into inch-long pieces

DUCK BREASTS WITH SWEET JERSEY CORN AND BACON

We use superb Long Island ducks, raised by the Corwin family on their 400-year-old Crescent Farm. But the corn is Jersey all the way. We especially love Sugar Pearl and Silver King varieties.

SERVES 4

FOR THE DUCK
AND DUCK SAUCE:

2 whole ducks (5 pounds each)

1 tablespoon extra-virgin
    olive oil

1 onion, chopped

1 carrot, chopped

1 celery rib, chopped

¾ cup button mushrooms,
    thinly sliced

2 shallots, chopped

2 teaspoons freshly ground
    black pepper

2 cups Chicken Stock
    (page 195)

1 cup veal demiglace

1 bunch fresh thyme

FOR THE CORN, LEEKS
AND BACON:

2 tablespoons extra-virgin
    olive oil

4 ounces smoked bacon, diced

1 pound leeks, thinly sliced

Kosher salt and freshly ground
    black pepper

4 tablespoons unsalted butter

2 fresh thyme sprigs

6 ears fresh sweet corn

1 cup water

1 tablespoon chopped flat-leaf
    parsley leaves

1 tablespoon minced chives

Rinse the ducks and pat dry. With a boning knife, cut the legs from each duck and reserve for another use.

Remove each duck breast from the carcass, leaving the skin on the meat. You will have 4 individual breasts. Using a sharp knife, cut a ¼-inch crosshatch pattern in the skin of each breast, being careful not to pierce the meat. Refrigerate breasts while making the sauce.

Remove excess fat from duck carcasses and cut carcasses into smaller pieces. Heat the oil in a large saucepan over moderate heat. Add the carcasses and cook, stirring occasionally, until browned, about 15 minutes. Add the onions, carrots and celery and cook, until golden brown, about 10 minutes. Add the mushrooms, shallots and black pepper and cook for 2 minutes. Stir in the chicken stock, demiglace and thyme and bring to a boil.

Lower the heat and simmer until sauce is reduced by half, 45 minutes to 1 hour. Strain through a fine-mesh sieve and refrigerate.

To make the corn, cook bacon in a large sauté pan over moderate heat, stirring occasionally, until crisp, about 8 minutes. Drain on a paper towel. Pour the drippings through a fine-mesh sieve into a small bowl.

Heat 2 tablespoons drippings in the cleaned pan over moderately high heat. Add leeks and season with salt and pepper. Cook about 5 minutes. Add 2 tablespoons butter and thyme and cook for 3 minutes. Transfer to a bowl, and wipe out the pan.

Cut kernels from ears of corn. Place half of the corn in a blender and purée with ½ cup water. Strain purée through a fine-mesh sieve into the top of a double boiler and reserve.

Melt the remaining 2 tablespoons butter in the large sauté pan over moderate heat. Add reserved corn kernels and remaining ½ cup water and season with salt and pepper. Cook, stirring occasionally, until the corn is almost tender, about 8 minutes.

Set the corn purée over simmering water and cook gently over low heat until the liquid thickens to the consistency of heavy cream, 3 to 4 minutes. Season with salt and pepper. Stir into the corn kernels. Add the cooked bacon, leeks and parsley. Taste and adjust the seasonings; keep warm until ready to use.

Season duck breasts with salt and pepper. Heat a sauté pan over moderate heat and add the breasts, skin side down. Cook until browned, about 10 minutes. Spoon out excess fat then turn and cook 4 minutes more for medium-rare. Remove from the pan and let sit for 5 minutes. Gently reheat the duck sauce.

To serve, spoon creamed corn on 4 warm plates. Thinly slice duck breasts and arrange over the corn. Spoon warm duck sauce around each breast and garnish with chives.

CAVATELLI WITH DUCK CONFIT RAGU

SERVES 4

6 ounces butternut squash,
    peeled and seeded
2 tablespoons extra-virgin
    olive oil
2 shallots, minced
1 small bunch mustard greens
    or other bitter greens,
    washed well, ribs removed
    and leaves coarsely
    chopped (about 2 cups)
1 pound Confit Duck Legs
    (page 102), skinned and
    shredded

1 pound cavatelli pasta
1 cup Chicken Stock
    (page 195)
4 tablespoons unsalted butter,
    cut into ½-inch pieces
¼ cup freshly grated
    Parmigiano Reggiano,
    plus more for serving
1 tablespoon chopped fresh
    sage leaves

There's something very New Jersey about cavatelli pasta; it's a favorite among the state's Italian-Americans. In this satisfying dish, it's combined with savory confit duck and bitter greens, their robustness balanced by the addition of sweet squash and creamy cheese. If you have the duck confit all ready to go, this dish comes together very quickly.

Using a mandoline or a very sharp knife, cut the squash lengthwise into $\frac{1}{16}$-inch-thick slices. Heat the olive oil in a large saucepan over moderately high heat, then add the shallots and cook for 1 minute. Add the squash and cook, stirring occasionally, until it begins to soften, about 2 minutes. Add the greens and shredded duck meat and cook until the greens have wilted, about 1 minute.

Cook the pasta in a large pot of salted boiling water until just shy of al dente. Drain the pasta (reserve a cup or so of cooking water to loosen the sauce if needed) and add it to the pan with the vegetables and duck. Add the chicken stock and butter and simmer until the sauce has reduced slightly and coats the pasta, about 3 minutes.

Remove from the heat and add the cheese and sage; toss well. Serve immediately, with extra cheese on the side.

Most quails can be purchased semi-boneless—with backbone, rib cage and thigh bones removed; the wing bones and drumsticks remain intact. Prepared this way, they are very easy to cook. Try serving this heady autumnal dish with Castle Valley Mill Soft Polenta (page 138), if you like. We get our quail from Griggstown Farm in Princeton when available.

Preheat a grill over moderately high heat. Put the quail in a shallow dish or bowl and rub all over with the herbes de Provence and 1 tablespoon olive oil. Season with salt and pepper.

Heat the remaining 1 tablespoon olive oil in a large sauté pan over moderate heat. Add the shallots and cook, stirring occasionally, until tender and golden browned, about 5 minutes. Add the grapes and cook until they release much of their liquid, about 5 minutes, then add the apple cider, stirring and scraping up any browned bits on the bottom of the pan, and simmer until slightly reduced. Stir in the chestnuts and cook until warmed through. Season with salt and pepper. Whisk in the butter, if you like, and remove from the heat. Set aside, covered, to keep warm.

Grill the quail, turning once, about 3 minutes per side for medium. Remove the quail from the grill and let rest for 2 minutes before serving.

To serve, cut the quails in half lengthwise and arrange 2 halves, crossed over each other, on each of 4 warmed plates. Spoon the warm grapes and chestnuts over the quails and garnish with the thyme leaves.

GRILLED QUAIL WITH GRAPES AND CHESTNUTS

SERVES 4

4 semiboneless quail
1½ teaspoons herbes de Provence
2 tablespoons extra-virgin olive oil
Kosher salt and freshly ground black pepper
5 shallots, thinly sliced

1 cup red grapes, halved
1 cup apple cider
¼ cup shelled roasted chestnuts, sliced
1 tablespoon unsalted butter (optional)
1 tablespoon fresh thyme leaves

CONFIT DUCK LEGS

MAKES 10 CONFIT DUCK LEGS

1 cup kosher salt

1 tablespoon freshly ground
    black pepper

Leaves from 4 fresh thyme
    sprigs

2 bay leaves, crumbled

1 teaspoon ground allspice

10 duck legs

2 to 3 quarts duck fat

We generally pull the confited duck meat off the bone before storing it in fat; that way, it's all ready to use in pasta (Cavatelli with Duck Confit Ragu, page 98) or to top a flatbread (Duck Confit Flatbread with Turnips, Goat Cheese and Caramelized Onion, page 62). If you prefer to keep it on the bone, you will need a larger amount of duck fat to preserve it.

Combine the salt, pepper, thyme leaves, bay leaves and allspice in a bowl. Rub the seasonings all over the duck legs. Place the seasoned duck legs in a container, cover and refrigerate for 24 hours.

Preheat the oven to 250°F. Remove the legs from the salt mixture, rinse under cold water and pat dry with paper towels.

Heat the duck fat in a large pot over low heat until it melts. Arrange the duck legs in 2 snug layers in a large ovenproof casserole dish or Dutch oven. Pour enough of the melted fat over the legs to cover them by 1 inch. Heat the casserole dish over moderately low heat until the fat comes to a gentle simmer. Transfer to the oven and bake, tightly covered, until the meat is very tender and is almost falling off the bone, 2½ to 3 hours.

Carefully remove the legs from the fat and pull the skin off (discard or save for another use). Pull the meat apart in large pieces and cool completely. Discard the bones. Transfer the cooled duck meat to a container. Carefully pour the duck fat through a fine-mesh sieve set over the duck meat just to cover. Cool completely, then cover tightly and store in the refrigerator for up to 2 weeks.

FROM THE CHEF
Salt: Coarse and Coarser

Traditionally used for koshering, or salting, meat to remove blood and impurities to conform with Jewish doctrine, kosher salt is a favorite of chefs who like it because the large crystals are easy to grab and their jagged shape sticks well to food. We use Diamond Crystal kosher salt in the Agricola kitchen, which is less dense than other brands. This is the salt we reach for when seasoning steaks before throwing them on the grill, salting pasta water, making a brine...really, almost anything.

But when we're finishing a dish, it's sea salt we want. We get ours from the Maine Sea Salt Company, which transfers seawater from the Gulf of Maine to greenhouses where it evaporates naturally until the remaining salt crystallizes. This flaky sea salt adds not only a pop of brine but a bit of welcome crunch to a finished dish.

To cook the guinea hen legs, preheat the oven to 250°F. Season the legs with salt and pepper. Heat 2 tablespoons olive oil in a sauté pan over high heat. Add the legs and cook until golden brown, about 4 minutes per side.

Pour the duck fat into a small pot, along with the fresh thyme, bay leaves and crushed garlic. Submerge the guinea hen legs in the fat. Heat over moderately low heat to just below a simmer. Remove from the heat, cover the pot, and put in the oven. Cook until the meat is very tender and almost falling off the bone, about 2 hours. Carefully remove the legs from the fat, then gently remove the bones, keeping the meat intact. Carefully return the leg meat to the duck fat mixture and reserve.

To make the farro and escarole, heat 2 tablespoons olive oil in a large saucepan over moderate heat. Add the red onion and cook, stirring occasionally, until deep golden brown, 8 to 10 minutes. Season with salt and pepper. Add the farro to the pan and cook, stirring, until toasted and fragrant. Add 4 cups vegetable stock and bring to a boil, then reduce the heat and simmer until the farro is tender, about 20 minutes. Remove from the heat and season the farro mixture with salt and pepper.

Season the guinea hen breasts with salt and pepper. Heat 2 tablespoons olive oil in a large sauté pan over high heat, add the breasts skin side down and sear until caramelized, 5 to 6 minutes. Flip and cook 7 minutes more. Remove from the pan and cover loosely with aluminum foil to keep warm.

Heat the butter and remaining 1 tablespoon olive oil in a large sauté pan over moderate heat. Add the escarole and cook, stirring occasionally, until lightly caramelized, about 8 minutes. Add the escarole to the farro and onion mixture. Return the sauté pan to the heat and deglaze it with the remaining 1 cup vegetable stock, stirring and scraping the bottom of the pan to loosen any browned bits. Stir the stock into the farro, then gently fold in orange segments, olives and oregano.

To serve, carefully transfer the guinea hen legs to a cutting board and chop the legs into 4 portions. Slice the guinea hen breasts. Divide the toasted farro and escarole among 4 warm plates. Top with a portion of the legs and sliced breasts and garnish with fresh parsley.

ROASTED GUINEA HEN WITH TOASTED FARRO AND ESCAROLE

Josh began cooking this dish when he lived in California, for a dinner at Tres Sabores Winery in Napa Valley. The winery, owned by Julie Johnson, has been organically certified since 1987. Not only does Julie produce amazing wines, she raises happy guinea hens that peck and scratch through her lemon and olive groves. In this preparation, the legs are confited and the breasts are seared. (Save the carcass to make stock.) The delicious farro with escarole goes well with roast chicken, seared duck breasts, or almost any poultry.

SERVES 4

1 guinea hen, 3½ to 4 pounds, breasts and legs separated (keep skin attached)
Kosher salt and freshly ground black pepper
7 tablespoons extra-virgin olive oil
4 cups duck fat, melted
1 bunch fresh thyme
2 bay leaves
1 garlic clove, crushed
1 medium red onion, finely chopped
2 cups dried farro

5 cups Vegetable Stock (page 194)
3 tablespoons unsalted butter
2 small heads escarole, torn into bite-sized pieces
1½ tablespoons finely chopped kalamata olives
1 valencia orange, peeled and segmented
1 teaspoon chopped oregano leaves
1 tablespoon chopped flat-leaf parsley leaves

BRAISED RABBIT WITH BACON, MORELS AND PEARL ONIONS

This rabbit is prepared in two ways: the legs are cooked low and slow with stock, wine and plenty of vegetables to make a rich, deeply flavored stew. The loins are wrapped with bacon and seared, then served over the braised meat along with buttery morels and onions.

SERVES 4 TO 6

2 rabbits, about 3 pounds each
4 thin slices smoked bacon
¼ cup plus 3 tablespoons
    extra-virgin olive oil
Kosher salt and freshly ground
    black pepper
1 cup dry red wine
2 celery ribs, finely chopped
1 onion, finely chopped
1 carrot, finely chopped
2 tablespoons tomato paste

4 fresh thyme sprigs
4 cups Chicken Stock
    (page 195), or as needed
1 tablespoon unsalted butter
2 large shallots, minced
1 cup morel mushrooms, sliced
1 cup pearl onions, peeled
1 tablespoon chopped flat-leaf
    parsley leaves
Castle Valley Mill Soft Polenta
    (page 138)

Cut the rabbits into 6 pieces each: 2 hind legs, 2 front legs and the saddle, which is cut into 2 loin pieces. Wrap the bacon strips around the loin pieces and set aside.

Heat 2 tablespoons olive oil in a large, deep sauté pan over moderately high heat. Season the rabbit legs with salt and pepper. Working in 2 batches, brown the rabbit (except the loin pieces), turning occasionally, until crisp and golden brown all over, 6 to 8 minutes (reduce the heat to moderate for the second batch). Transfer the rabbit to a large plate.

Add the wine to the pan and cook over moderately high heat for about 1 minute, stirring and scraping up any browned bits on the bottom of the pan. Pour the wine into a cup; wipe out the skillet.

Add ¼ cup olive oil to the pan. Add the celery, onions and carrots and cook over moderate heat, stirring occasionally, until softened, 8 to 10 minutes. Add the tomato paste and thyme and cook, stirring constantly, until the tomato paste begins to brown, 3 to 4 minutes. Add the reserved wine to the pan and cook, stirring occasionally, until sizzling, about 1 minute. Add the rabbit and any accumulated juices to the pan, along with 2 cups chicken stock (or enough to reach about halfway up the side of the pan) and bring to a boil. Reduce the heat to low, cover partially and simmer for 30 minutes. Add the remaining 2 cups stock and cook until the sauce is slightly reduced and the rabbit is tender, about 20 minutes longer. Remove the rabbit from the pot, cover to keep warm, and discard the thyme sprigs. Continue to simmer the sauce until reduced to about 1½ cups, about 8 minutes. Remove from the heat and return the rabbit to the skillet and keep warm.

Heat the remaining tablespoon of olive oil in a medium sauté pan over moderately high heat. Add the bacon-wrapped rabbit loins and cook, turning gently, until golden brown all over, about 8 minutes. Remove from the heat and let rest, loosely covered with foil, for 5 minutes.

Meanwhile, heat the butter in a medium sauté pan over moderately high heat. Add the shallots, morels and pearl onions and cook, stirring occasionally, until the mushrooms are tender, about 8 minutes. Season to taste with salt and pepper.

To serve, slice each bacon-wrapped loin into 4 pieces. Arrange the rabbit stew on a large platter and top with the sliced loins. Spoon the mushrooms and onions over the rabbit and garnish with chopped parsley. Serve with soft polenta on the side.

TRUFFLE CHICKEN BREASTS WITH CELERY ROOT RÉMOULADE

SERVES 4

1 large celery root (about 1¼ pounds), trimmed and peeled

2 tablespoons freshly squeezed lemon juice

Kosher salt and freshly ground black pepper

½ cup mayonnaise

2 tablespoons Dijon mustard

1 tablespoon capers, rinsed and chopped

2 tablespoons extra-virgin olive oil

4 large boneless organic chicken breasts, skin on

1 tablespoon truffle butter

4 fresh thyme sprigs

1 cup Pickled Red Beets (page 177), for serving

Part of our mission at Agricola is to support both local food-based charities and culinary professional development. We've worked closely with the Culinary Arts Program at Mercer County Community College, and sponsored a scholarship there to help advance the next generation of chefs. Josh created this dish when he was teaching a class at MCCC, and it's one of those fantastic combinations that tastes very luxe but is incredibly simple to pull together. We serve it with pickled beets.

To make the rémoulade, cut the celery root into thin matchsticks. Combine the celery root with 1 tablespoon lemon juice and season well with salt and pepper. Stir together the mayonnaise, mustard, capers and remaining tablespoon of lemon juice in a small bowl, then add to the celery root and toss to combine thoroughly. Let sit while you cook the chicken.

To cook the chicken, heat the olive oil in a large sauté pan over moderately high heat. Season the chicken breasts all over with salt and pepper, then add, skin side down, to the pan. Cook for 2 to 3 minutes, then reduce the heat to moderate and cook until the skin is crisp and golden brown, about 10 minutes. Flip the breasts and add the truffle butter and thyme to the pan. Continue to cook, basting the chicken with the pan juices, until cooked through, 8 to 10 minutes. Remove the chicken from the pan and let rest, loosely covered, for few minutes.

Taste the celery root rémoulade and adjust the seasonings as needed. Make a small pile of rémoulade and a small pile of pickled beets on each of 4 plates. Slice the chicken breasts, arrange the meat between the vegetables, and spoon the pan juices over the chicken.

We always have a dish on our menu that is served family style, and this fried chicken has become a favorite of both guests and staff. In place of the expected mashed potatoes, we like to serve it with nutritious rutabagas mashed with butter and a dash of nutmeg. (See recipe, page 139.)

Combine the lemons, thyme, 1 cup salt, 1 cup sugar and 1 gallon water in a large pot and bring to a boil. Boil, stirring, until the salt and sugar are dissolved. Remove from the heat and cool completely.

Cut the chicken into 10 pieces: 2 drumsticks, 2 thighs, 2 wings and 2 halved breasts. Add all the chicken to the cold brine, cover, and refrigerate for 8 hours or overnight.

Remove the chicken from the brine, rinse under cold water, and pat dry with paper towels.

Whisk together the flour, garlic powder, onion powder, paprika, cayenne, black pepper and remaining 1½ teaspoons salt in a bowl. Pour the buttermilk into a second bowl. Dredge the chicken pieces in the flour mixture, shaking off the excess, then dip in the buttermilk, then dredge again in the flour mixture. Set aside on a tray.

Fill a large, deep pot ⅓ full with canola oil. Heat the oil to 320°F. Carefully place the chicken thighs and legs into the hot oil and cook, flipping occasionally, until golden brown and crisp, about 12 minutes. Using tongs, remove the thighs and legs and drain on a paper towel–lined rack. Repeat with the other pieces of chicken. The heat of the oil will drop when all the chicken is in the pot; you might have to increase the heat to maintain the temperature. Breasts will take about 7 minutes to fry. Wings take about 6 minutes to fry.

We like to serve this chicken, sprinkled with coarse salt, on a warmed serving platter lined with a cloth napkin.

FRIED CHICKEN

SERVES 2 TO 4

2 lemons, halved
1 bunch fresh thyme
1 cup plus 1½ teaspoons
    kosher salt
1 cup sugar
1 (3-pound) chicken
3 cups all-purpose flour
2 tablespoons garlic powder

2 tablespoons onion powder
1½ teaspoons paprika
1½ teaspoons cayenne pepper
1½ teaspoon freshly ground
    black pepper
2 cups buttermilk
Canola oil, for frying

CHICKEN POT PIES

FOR THE CRUST:

2 cups all-purpose flour

½ teaspoon kosher salt

12 tablespoons (1½ sticks)
cold unsalted butter, cut
into ½-inch pieces

4 to 8 tablespoons ice water

1 large egg (for egg wash)

FOR THE FILLING:

4 tablespoons unsalted butter

¼ cup all-purpose flour

6 cups Chicken Stock
(page 195)

1 whole clove

1 small onion, peeled

1 bay leaf

Kosher salt and freshly ground
white pepper

1 large russet potato, peeled
and diced

8 ounces carrots, diced

1¼ pounds boneless, skinless
chicken breasts, cut into
¾-inch dice

5 tablespoons olive oil

12 ounces mixed mushrooms,
such as cremini and
shiitake, sliced

1 cup fresh corn kernels

1 cup shelled peas

1 tablespoon fresh thyme
leaves

2¼ cups heavy cream

1 tablespoon chopped flat-leaf
parsley leaves

EQUIPMENT:

4 (5-inch) soufflé dishes

A homemade chicken pot pie is a fine thing to behold, topped in flaky golden pastry and exuding delicious aromas. Using good homemade chicken stock for the gravy is what makes this homey dish so special. If you have access to fresh sweet peas from the garden or farm market, the pie will be that much more of a treat. The pastry can be made a day in advance.

To make the crust, put the flour and salt in a small bowl and cut in the butter with your fingertips or a pastry blender just until the mixture resembles coarse meal with some pea-sized lumps of butter. Add 4 tablespoons water and quickly stir until incorporated, adding more water, 1 tablespoon at a time, until the dough just comes together. Gather into a ball, flatten into a disk, and wrap tightly with plastic wrap. Refrigerate for at least 30 minutes and up to overnight.

To make the filling, melt the butter in a heavy saucepan over moderate heat. Just as it starts to bubble, add the flour and cook, stirring constantly, for 2 minutes. Slowly whisk in the chicken stock. Stick the clove into the onion and add to the stock with the bay leaf. Bring to a simmer and cook, stirring occasionally, for 30 minutes. Season the gravy with salt and white pepper. Remove the onion and bay leaf.

Meanwhile, cook the diced potatoes and carrots in a medium saucepan of salted boiling water until they begin to soften, about 5 minutes. Drain well and set aside.

Preheat the oven to 375°F. Season the chicken with salt and pepper. Heat 4 tablespoons of the olive oil in a large sauté pan over high heat. Working in batches so as not to crowd the pan, cook the chicken until golden brown, about 5 minutes (the chicken will not be fully cooked). Remove from the heat and divide the chicken evenly among the soufflé dishes.

Add the remaining tablespoon of oil to the same pan and cook the mushrooms, stirring occasionally, until golden brown, about 8 minutes. Stir in the corn, peas, reserved potatoes and carrots, and thyme. Season the vegetables with salt and pepper and divide evenly among the soufflé dishes.

Add the gravy to the same pan and simmer over moderately high heat until thickened and reduced by a third, about 5 minutes. Add the cream, reduce the heat, and simmer gently until reduced by half, about 15 minutes. Stir in the parsley and season to taste. Pour the gravy over the vegetables and chicken.

Remove the dough from the refrigerator and roll out into a ¹⁄₁₆-inch-thick circle on a lightly floured surface. Cut out four 6-inch circles of dough (which will allow for a ½-inch overhang for each baking dish). Top each dish with a circle of pie dough, pressing the overhang against the side of the dish to seal. Beat the egg with 1 tablespoon water in a small bowl, and brush the tops of the dough with the egg wash. Cut a few steam vent holes in the dough.

Place the dishes on a baking sheet and bake until golden brown, about 45 minutes. Let the pies rest for 5 to 10 minutes before serving.

Freshly ground beef, housemade buns and a bevy of vegetables—this is one of the dishes that truly speaks to who we are. If you want to follow our lead, buy whole brisket, cut the meat into chunks, and grind it twice using a well-chilled meat grinder (a warm grinder will melt the fat, smearing it through the meat). The first time, the meat should go through the coarse plate of the grinder, then through the fine plate. And it shouldn't be too lean—18 percent fat is ideal.

It's tempting for cooks to want to season the meat with onion, garlic and spices, but if you're using good-quality beef, the accompaniments will add all the extra flavor you need. The summer squash pickles are an homage to those served on burgers at the great Zuni Café in San Francisco. We always serve Handcut Potato Fries (page 141) on the side, along with a jar of our Red Beet Ketchup (page 182).

Heat a grill to moderate heat. Using your hands, shape the cold ground beef into 4 patties, about ½-inch thick. Handle the beef as quickly and gently as possible; "kneading" the meat can result in tough, dry burgers. Brush both sides of the patties lightly with olive oil and season with salt and pepper. Brush the grill lightly with olive oil and grill the burgers over a moderate flame until done to your preference (5 to 6 minutes per side for medium rare; 7 to 8 minutes per side for medium; 9 to 10 minutes per side for well done).

Meanwhile, cut the buns in half and place on the grill to toast lightly, then transfer to warm plates. Top the bottom buns with a lettuce leaf and a burger. Top the burgers with the cheese and pickles. Spread the aïoli over the top of the bun's cut side and arrange on top of the dressed burger.

AGRICOLA BURGER

SERVES 4

2 pounds ground brisket
Extra-virgin olive oil, for brushing
Kosher salt and freshly ground black pepper
4 Hamburger Buns (see recipe, page 114)
4 Little Gem or romaine lettuce leaves

4 slices cheese, preferably a flavorful cows' milk cheese such as fontina
Quick Pickled Zucchini and Squash (page 174)
4 tablespoons Herb Aïoli (page 114)

HAMBURGER BUNS

Topped with bits of sautéed onions, these buns are something special. Extra buns may be frozen for up to 1 month. You can also freeze the unbaked rolls, before proofing, on a baking sheet and then transfer to a plastic bag. When ready to use, simply thaw the dough, let it proof, and bake as directed below.

MAKES 12 BUNS

1¼ cups whole milk, warmed
4½ teaspoons active dry yeast
3½ cups bread flour
⅓ cup granulated sugar
2 large eggs

4 tablespoons unsalted butter, softened
1 tablespoon kosher salt
1 teaspoon extra-virgin olive oil
¼ cup finely diced onions

Combine the milk and yeast in the bowl of a stand mixer and let sit until the yeast is dissolved and foamy, about 5 minutes.

Add the flour, sugar, 1 egg, butter and salt to the yeast mixture and mix with the dough hook attachment until the dough is smooth and pulls away from the sides of the bowl, about 8 minutes.

Transfer the dough to a large buttered bowl and let rest, covered with plastic wrap, until doubled in size, about 2 hours.

Preheat the oven to 400°F. Dump out the dough onto a floured work surface and divide into 12 equal pieces. Shape the dough into rolls, place on a greased or parchment-lined baking sheet and drape lightly with plastic wrap. Let the dough proof in a warm spot until just about doubled in size, about 30 minutes.

While the dough proofs, heat the olive oil in a small sauté pan over moderately high heat. Add the onions and cook, stirring occasionally, until golden, 5 to 8 minutes. Remove from the heat.

Lightly beat the remaining egg and brush the tops of the rolls with the egg wash. Sprinkle the sautéed onions over the rolls. Bake until golden brown, rotating the sheet pan halfway through, about 15 minutes. Let cool.

HERB AÏOLI

This simple garlic mayonnaise, flecked with parsley and chives, tastes good on just about everything.

MAKES ABOUT 1 CUP

1 large garlic clove
Kosher salt
1 large egg yolk
1 cup extra-virgin olive oil

Freshly ground black pepper
1½ teaspoons minced chives
1½ teaspoons minced flat-leaf parsley leaves

Finely chop the garlic, then sprinkle with a pinch of salt and continue chopping and mashing until the mixture forms a paste. Transfer the garlic paste to a bowl with the egg yolk and whisk together. Slowly add the oil in a thin stream, whisking constantly until thickened and very creamy. Season the aïoli with salt and pepper and fold in the minced herbs. Refrigerate, covered, until ready to use.

FAMILY MEAL MEAT LOAF WITH BARBECUE SAUCE

This is the kind of dish we like to serve for the staff's family meal—big, pleasing flavors that are also supremely comforting. If you're not feeding such a large crowd, the recipe can be easily cut in half. Any leftovers are delicious the next day, stuffed cold into a sandwich with lettuce and mayo.

SERVES 12 TO 16 HUNGRY STAFF

2 pounds ground beef

2 pounds ground veal

1 pound ground pork

4 large eggs

1 cup finely chopped fresh tomato

1 cup panko

¾ cup chopped flat-leaf parsley leaves

½ cup chopped chives

2 tablespoons minced basil leaves

4 teaspoons kosher salt

1 tablespoon freshly ground black pepper

1 cup Barbecue Sauce (see below)

8 slices smoked bacon

Whipped Yukon Golds (page 139), for serving

Preheat the oven to 350°F. In a large bowl, gently mix together the beef, veal, pork, eggs, tomato, panko, parsley, chives, basil, salt and pepper. Take care not to overwork the mixture.

Divide the mixture between two 12-inch-long loaf pans. Brush ½ cup barbecue sauce over the top of each loaf, then arrange the bacon strips over the tops of the meatloaves.

Bake until a meat thermometer inserted in the center of each meatloaf registers 145°F, 1 to 1½ hours. Let cool slightly, then carefully lift the meat loaves from the pans, slice and serve with the whipped potatoes.

BARBECUE SAUCE

MAKES ABOUT 6 CUPS

1 tablespoon grapeseed oil

1 yellow onion, chopped

2 garlic cloves, chopped

1 small jalapeño, stemmed, seeded and minced

1 dried ancho chile, stemmed and crumbled

4 pounds fresh tomatoes, ground, or two (28-ounce) cans whole tomatoes, ground

1 cup tomato juice

1 cup ketchup

½ cup molasses

½ cup red wine vinegar

¼ cup Dijon mustard

2 tablespoons Worcestershire sauce

2 tablespoons packed light brown sugar

1½ tablespoons hot sauce, such as Tabasco

1½ teaspoons Chinese five-spice powder

Heat the grapeseed oil in a large saucepan over moderate heat. Add the onion and cook, stirring occasionally, until deeply golden, about 15 minutes. Add the garlic, jalapeño and crumbled ancho chile and cook, stirring, until fragrant but not browned, 1 to 2 minutes. Add the remaining ingredients and bring to a simmer. Cook, stirring occasionally, until thickened and reduced, about 1 hour. Remove from the heat and, working in batches, purée in a blender (use caution when blending hot liquids). Cool completely then refrigerate in an airtight container until ready to use. The barbecue sauce will keep for several weeks in the refrigerator.

This soup deserves to be made at the height of summer, when tomatoes are at their juiciest.

ROASTED TOMATO SOUP WITH GRILLED MOZZARELLA SANDWICHES

SERVES 4

To make the soup, preheat the oven to 325°F. Gently toss the tomatoes with 4 tablespoons olive oil in a bowl, season with salt and pepper, and arrange in a roasting pan. Scatter the thyme sprigs over the tomatoes. Roast the tomatoes until collapsed and very fragrant, about 1½ hours.

Meanwhile, heat the remaining 2 tablespoons olive oil in a heavy pot over moderately high heat. Add the onions and garlic and cook, stirring occasionally, until deeply golden, about 10 minutes. Season with salt and pepper.

Scrape the roasted tomatoes and their juices into the onion mixture in the pot. Reduce the heat to low and cook, stirring occasionally and making sure the mixture is not burning, for 45 minutes.

Remove the tomato mixture from the heat and purée in a blender until very smooth. Stir in the basil leaves. Keep warm.

To make the sandwiches, arrange the slices of mozzarella on 4 slices of bread. Top with the remaining bread. Brush both sides of the sandwiches with the oil.

Preheat a sauté pan or a sandwich press over moderately low heat and cook the sandwiches until golden brown on one side, about 4 minutes. Flip the sandwiches and continue to cook until the second side is golden brown and the cheese has melted, about 4 minutes more.

To serve, divide the soup among 4 small warm bowls, garnish with some of the reserved basil leaves, and serve the sandwiches on the side.

FOR THE SOUP:

4 pounds ripe heirloom tomatoes, halved
6 tablespoons extra-virgin olive oil
Kosher salt and freshly ground black pepper
8 fresh thyme sprigs
1 large white onion, finely chopped
4 garlic cloves, minced
1 cup fresh basil leaves, plus extra for garnish

FOR THE SANDWICHES:

6 ounces Fresh Mozzarella (page 118), thinly sliced
Eight ½-inch slices ciabatta or bread of your choice
2 tablespoons extra-virgin olive oil

How to Make Fresh Mozzarella

Measure out 1 cup water. Stir in 1½ teaspoons citric acid until dissolved. Measure out ¼ cup water in a separate bowl. Add ¼ rennet tablet (or ¼ teaspoon liquid rennet) and stir until dissolved.

Pour 1 gallon whole or 2% milk (not ultrapasteurized) into a pot. Stir in the citric acid solution. Set the pot over moderately high heat and warm to 90°F, stirring gently.

Remove the pot from the heat and gently stir in the rennet solution. Count to 30, stirring constantly. Stop stirring, then cover the pot and let sit, undisturbed, for 5 minutes.

After 5 minutes, the milk should have set, and it should look and feel like silken tofu. If the milk is still liquidy, cover the pot again and let it sit for another 5 minutes. Once the milk has set, cut it into uniform curds by making several parallel cuts vertically through the curds and then several parallel cuts horizontally, creating a grid-like pattern. Make sure your knife reaches all the way to the bottom of the pan.

Place the pot back on the stove over moderate heat and warm the curds to 105°F. Stir slowly as the curds warm, but try not to break them up too much.

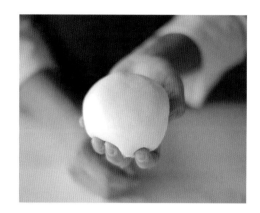

The curds will eventually clump together and separate more completely from the yellow whey.

Remove the pan from the heat and continue stirring gently for another 5 minutes.

Ladle the curds into a bowl with the slotted spoon.

Warm a large pot of water to just below boiling (about 190°F). Pour the curds into a strainer and nestle the strainer into the pot so the curds are submerged in the hot water. Let the curds sit for about 5 minutes. Wearing rubber gloves, fold the curds under the water and check their internal temperature. If it has not reached 135°F, let the curds sit for another few minutes until it does. Once they have reached 135°, lift them from the water.

Sprinkle 1 teaspoon kosher salt over the cheese and squish it with your fingers to incorporate. Using both hands, stretch and fold the curds repeatedly. It will start to tighten, become firm, and take on a glossy sheen. When this happens, you are ready to shape the mozzarella. Make one large ball or two smaller balls, taking care not to overwork the mozzarella.

The mozzarella can be used immediately or kept refrigerated for a week. To refrigerate, place the mozzarella in a small container. Mix 1 teaspoon kosher salt with a cup of the cooled whey and pour this over the mozzarella. Cover and refrigerate until ready to use.

POACHED EGGS "ARE NOT JUST FOR BREAKFAST"

SERVES 4

8 small potatoes, such as
    fingerlings
12 medium green asparagus
    stalks
1 head frisée lettuce
2 tablespoons distilled white
    vinegar
4 large organic eggs

2 tablespoons extra-virgin
    olive oil
Kosher salt and freshly ground
    black pepper
1 tablespoon minced chives
1 fresh black truffle, optional

When Josh was writing the first menu for Agricola, he wanted to find a way to showcase the amazing eggs from Great Road Farm's hens, but at the time we were only opening the restaurant for dinner. This is one of the first ideas he had, one that is perfect in its simplicity.

Combine the potatoes with cold salted water to cover in a saucepan. Bring to a boil then reduce the heat and simmer until tender, about 15 minutes. Drain well and set aside.

Prepare an ice water bath. Cook the asparagus in a medium pot of boiling salted water until tender, about 4 minutes. Using tongs, gently transfer the asparagus to the ice water bath to stop the cooking process. Drain on a kitchen towel and set aside.

Clean the frisée by picking out the tender, innermost yellow-white stems, reserving the outer green leaves for another use.

To poach the eggs, fill a deep pot with 5 inches of water. Add the vinegar and bring to a boil then reduce the heat to a simmer. Break one egg at a time into a small cup then gently slip the egg into the hot water. Working quickly, repeat with the remaining eggs, spacing them out in the pot. Once all the eggs are in, remove the pot from the heat and let the eggs stand until the whites are firm and the yolks are still liquid, about 4 minutes.

While the eggs are standing, heat the olive oil in a sauté pan over moderate heat. Add the potatoes and asparagus and cook, tossing occasionally, until warmed through, about 3 minutes. Season with salt and pepper.

Divide the potatoes and asparagus among 4 warmed plates and top with a small nest of frisée. Sprinkle with chives.

When the eggs are ready, use a slotted spoon to scoop them out of the water one at a time, blot them on a kitchen towel and place one on each nest of lettuce. Season the eggs with pepper. Using a truffle slicer or mandoline, thinly shave the truffle over the eggs, if you like, and serve at once.

The combination of Great Road Farm eggs and silky smoked salmon from our friend Max Hansen is as close to perfection as you can get. Max, who works out of Bucks County, makes some of the best smoked salmon we've ever tasted. To ensure the eggs have the right consistency, you must cook them over low heat, stirring constantly.

Beat the eggs in a bowl until blended. Season with ½ teaspoon salt and a bit of pepper.

Melt the butter in a nonstick sauté pan over low heat. Add the eggs and, using a rubber spatula, stir gently until they just begin to set. Add the smoked salmon and stir until warmed through, about 30 seconds.

When the eggs are softly set, remove the pan from the heat, and gently fold in the mascarpone. Be careful not to overmix; you should still see white streaks of mascarpone through the eggs. Transfer the eggs to a warm serving platter, garnish with chives and serve at once, with buttered toast on the side.

SOFT SCRAMBLED EGGS WITH MAX'S SMOKED SALMON

SERVES 4

12 large eggs
Kosher salt and freshly ground
  black pepper
2 tablespoons unsalted butter
8 ounces smoked salmon, cut
  into small pieces

⅔ cup mascarpone cheese
1 tablespoon minced chives
Toasted and buttered country-
  style bread, for serving

FROM THE FARMER
Eggs: Hens on the Run

Just up the hill from our vegetable barn are two large wooden chicken coops surrounded by a fenced-in run, home to our flock of 200 hens. About half are a cross between White Rocks and Rhode Island Reds, from a local breeder; they are very good producers of brown eggs. The other half are Silver Laced Wyandottes, known for their hardiness, which keeps them laying well all winter. It's important to have different breeds for diversity's sake and, practically, for culling purposes.

Most hens lay well—an egg every day to day and a half—for about two years. Once chickens stop laying, we can't afford to be sentimental and keep them around. I have a friend who slaughters them in exchange for some space in our greenhouse, and they become stewing chickens for the farm crew.

Chickens have to be cared for every day, no matter what. They need to be let out of their coops, fed, watered in the morning, and closed in at dusk. Eggs must be collected every day. We provide a non-GMO organic grain feed that is produced locally, but because chickens like to scratch, peck, and root around looking for bugs and insects, we also rotate them on pasture. And, of course, they get to feast on vegetable scraps from Agricola's kitchen (they love tomatoes!). All of this variety leads to spectacular eggs—the yolks are deep orange and just packed with flavor.

VEGETABLES

A BUMPER CROP OF SIDE DISHES

FAVA BEANS WITH GARLIC AND THYME

When baskets of fava beans appear at the market, you know that deep spring has arrived. Shelling the beans then peeling away the tough skin surrounding them takes a bit of time, but it's worth it for that tender, unmistakably bittersweet flavor. Blanching the favas quickly in salted water not only makes them easier to peel, it enhances and preserves their bright green color—after all, we know our guests eat with their eyes first. These beans are delicious with lamb or roast chicken, or served with our Gnocchi (page 74).

SERVES 4

5 pounds fresh fava beans in their pods
2 tablespoons extra-virgin olive oil
2 small garlic cloves, minced
1 tablespoon fresh thyme leaves
1 tablespoon unsalted butter
Kosher salt and freshly ground black pepper

Prepare an ice water bath. Bring a large pot of salted water to a boil while you shell the fava. Add the shelled fava beans to the boiling water and boil until bright green and tender, 1 to 2 minutes. Drain the beans and transfer to the ice water bath.

Drain the cooled fava beans in a colander. Peel off and discard the tough skin surrounding the beans.

Heat the olive oil in a large saucepan over moderate heat. Add the garlic and thyme leaves and cook, stirring occasionally, until golden and fragrant, about 2 minutes. Add the peeled favas and the butter and cook until the butter is melted and the beans are heated through, about 2 minutes. Remove from the heat and season to taste with salt and pepper.

SNAP PEAS AND TURNIPS WITH MINT AND PRESERVED LEMON

Slivers of preserved lemon add a briny yellow punch to this crisp, sweet salad that bespeaks Great Road Farm's early spring bounty. Quickly blanched, the turnips stay sweet and firm, enhanced by the grace note of fragrant fresh mint.

SERVES 4

1 pound sugar snap peas, trimmed
Kosher salt
¾ pound baby turnips, peeled and halved
2 teaspoons minced shallots
1 tablespoon freshly squeezed lemon juice
1 tablespoon champagne vinegar
¼ cup extra-virgin olive oil
1 Preserved Lemon (page 185), rind only, cut into very thin strips
2 tablespoons chopped fresh mint leaves
Sea salt and freshly ground black pepper, to taste

Prepare an ice water bath. Bring a large pot of water to a boil and season heavily with kosher salt. Add the snap peas to the boiling water and cook at a rolling boil for 15 seconds, then scoop out and immediately transfer the snap peas to the ice water to stop the cooking and preserve their color. After 2 minutes, drain the peas well and pat dry with paper towels. Refrigerate until ready to use.

Add the turnips to the pot of boiling water and cook for 90 seconds. Drain in a colander and add the turnips to the ice water bath to stop the cooking. When the turnips have cooled, drain them well and pat dry with kitchen towels.

Combine the shallots, lemon juice and vinegar in a large bowl. Gradually whisk in the olive oil to make the vinaigrette. Add the peas, turnips, preserved lemon and mint to the bowl. Mix the salad and season to taste with sea salt and pepper.

EGGPLANT CAPONATA

This classic Sicilian sweet and sour dish pairs well with fish, beef or lamb, but it's equally delicious slathered simply on some good crusty bread. Although the eggplant—unpeeled, for best texture and flavor—should be cut into generous 1-inch cubes, cut all the other vegetables into ½-inch dice.

SERVES 4 TO 6

1 large eggplant (about 1½ pounds), cut into 1-inch cubes
Kosher salt
½ cup extra-virgin olive oil
3 celery ribs, diced
½ fennel bulb, cored and diced
1 zucchini, diced
½ medium onion, diced
1 garlic clove, minced
2 medium ripe tomatoes, cored and diced

½ cup green olives, pitted and coarsely chopped
¼ cup capers, rinsed
¼ cup golden raisins
¼ cup pine nuts, toasted
¼ cup white wine vinegar
1 tablespoon sugar
Freshly ground black pepper
½ cup fresh basil leaves, very thinly sliced

Put the eggplant in a colander set over a bowl or the sink, sprinkle with 1 tablespoon salt and toss to coat. Let the eggplant sit and drain for 45 minutes to 1 hour. Rinse well and pat dry with paper towels.

Heat ¼ cup olive oil in a large pot over moderate heat. Add the celery and fennel and cook, stirring occasionally, for 2 minutes. Add the zucchini and cook for 3 minutes. Add the eggplant and cook, stirring occasionally, until the vegetables are golden brown and tender, about 10 minutes. Using a slotted spoon, transfer the vegetables to a plate lined with paper towels.

Add the remaining ¼ cup oil to the pot. Add the onions and garlic and cook over moderate heat until golden brown, about 6 minutes. Stir in the tomatoes, olives, capers, raisins, nuts, vinegar and sugar and cook, stirring occasionally, for 10 minutes. Return the eggplant, zucchini, celery and fennel to the pot and cook for 10 minutes more, stirring occasionally, taking care not to break up the eggplant too much. Season to taste with salt and pepper.

Remove from the heat and transfer the caponata to a shallow dish. Let cool to room temperature, then fold in the basil. Then take a deep breath: it's summer, and the basil smells heavenly.

RAINBOW SWISS CHARD WITH GARLIC AND LEMON

At our farm on nearby Great Road, we grow beautiful, robust Swiss chard. The rainbow varieties are our favorites—their bright pink, yellow, purple, orange and green stems look so handsome together on a plate. They're delicious on their own, but a little bacon never hurts!

SERVES 4

1 large bunch rainbow Swiss chard (about 1½ pounds)
3 tablespoons extra-virgin olive oil
4 strips smoked bacon, diced (optional)

2 garlic cloves, minced
Freshly squeezed juice of ½ lemon
Kosher salt and freshly ground black pepper

Using a sharp knife, cut the stems from the Swiss chard leaves. Dice the stems into 1-inch pieces; keep the leaves whole.

Prepare an ice water bath. Blanch the leaves in a large pot of boiling salted water for 1 minute. Using tongs or a slotted spoon, transfer the leaves to the ice bath. Pull the cooled leaves from the ice bath and drain well. Squeeze the extra liquid from the leaves and roughly chop. Set aside.

Add the chard stems to the boiling water and blanch for 2 minutes. Drain well and add to the ice bath. Drain the cooled stems well and pat dry with paper towels.

Heat the olive oil in a large sauté pan over moderately high heat. If you are using it, add the chopped bacon to the pan and cook, stirring occasionally, until golden brown and crisp, about 8 minutes. Add the garlic and cook until it starts to brown, about 1 minute. Add the chard stems and leaves and cook, stirring, for 3 minutes. Remove from the heat. Stir in the lemon juice and season to taste with salt and pepper.

ROASTED BELL PEPPERS

This colorful blend of bell peppers is as delicious at room temperature as it is hot from the skillet, so it can be made several hours ahead. When farmers' markets abound with peppers of all hues and varieties, it's even better.

SERVES 4

3 bell peppers, preferably a mix of colors
½ teaspoon balsamic vinegar
½ teaspoon red wine vinegar
2 tablespoons extra-virgin olive oil
2 garlic cloves, minced
2 teaspoons dried red chili flakes, or to taste
1 medium onion, halved and thinly sliced
Kosher salt and freshly ground black pepper
¼ cup fresh basil leaves, torn
1 tablespoon fresh oregano leaves

Roast the whole peppers on a grill or on the burner plate of a gas stove over an open flame, turning frequently, until the skins are blistered and charred all over. Put the blackened peppers in a paper bag and let them steam for about 15 minutes (this will help loosen the skins and make the peppers easier to peel).

Peel off and discard the peppers' skins. Cut out the stems and open up the peppers; scrape out the seeds and ribs. Cut the peppers into long strips and put in a bowl. Drizzle the vinegars over the peppers.

Heat the olive oil in a medium sauté pan over moderately high heat. Add the garlic and chili flakes and cook, stirring, for 1 minute. Add the onions and cook, stirring occasionally, until just beginning to soften, about 3 minutes. Remove from the heat and add the onions and garlic to the roasted peppers. Season to taste with salt and pepper, and scatter the basil and oregano over the peppers.

GRILLED CORN ON THE COB WITH SPICY LIME BUTTER

In July and August, sweet Jersey corn on the cob is so good that it needs little fussing. When you do want to gild the lily, this spicy lime butter adds a nice kick. The technique of wrapping the corn in foil before grilling ensures juicy, delicious results.

SERVES 4

½ cup (1 stick) unsalted butter, melted
1 tablespoon chopped cilantro leaves
1 teaspoon freshly squeezed lime juice
⅛ teaspoon cayenne pepper
4 fresh ears sweet corn, shucked and halved

Preheat a grill to moderately high heat. Combine the melted butter, cilantro, lime juice and cayenne in a small bowl.

Brush the butter mixture onto the ears of corn, then wrap tightly in aluminum foil. Grill the corn, turning often, until the kernels begin to char, about 15 minutes. Carefully unwrap the corn over a bowl to save the butter drippings.

Transfer the grilled corn to a serving platter and drizzle the melted butter over it.

Zone 7

Mikey Azzara is a guy who makes things happen. He's the spark of pure energy behind Zone 7, a distribution service that connects farms and restaurants in New Jersey and eastern Pennsylvania. Zone 7 supplies Agricola with almost everything we need that we can't get from our own Great Road Farm. It's a crucial link in keeping the food we serve as locally sourced as possible.

Mikey started farming after college and worked for the Northeast Organic Farming Association of New Jersey, where one of his projects was to connect farmers and chefs. "There was always a lot of excitement about working together," he remembers. "But when I would follow up with the farmers and chefs after the meeting, nine times out of ten they had not stayed connected." The reality of maintaining a true "farm to table" restaurant is incredibly difficult and time-consuming, and the idea of chefs strolling the greenmarket early in the morning is more often a romantic myth than reality. Nor do

most farmers have the time—between planting, weeding, harvesting, driving to farmers markets and maintaining a farmstand—to personally take orders from and deliver to restaurants.

In 2007, Mark and Judy Dornstreich of Branch Creek Farm in Bucks County invited Mikey out to their 21-acre farm, which has provided organic produce to top Philadelphia restaurants for some 30 years. "They sat me down and said, 'Distribution is the missing link, and we think you're the person to do it.' They offered me their truck and their son as a driver. They even gave me the name—Zone 7. They knew the farmers needed help."

So Mikey called ten farms and ten restaurants to see if they were interested in working with him, and they all said yes. Ironically, it's not so easy to be a true farm-to-table restaurant in the Garden State, but thanks to Zone 7, we're well on our way.

STUFFED ZUCCHINI BLOSSOMS WITH FRESH TOMATO SAUCE

You might find yourself eating these ricotta-stuffed blossoms like candy—they're that good. It's easy to double or triple this recipe, so fry up a batch, eat them fresh, then make more. Whether you buy zucchini flowers from the farmers' market or harvest them from your own garden, make sure to use them as soon as possible because they are an ephemeral treat.

SERVES 4

1½ cups fresh ricotta cheese
1 tablespoon thinly sliced fresh basil leaves
1 teaspoon freshly ground black pepper
12 large zucchini blossoms with stems intact
1½ cups all-purpose flour
1 teaspoon kosher salt
1 large egg, lightly beaten

2 cups club soda
1 tablespoon extra-virgin olive oil
Canola oil, for frying
4 to 6 fresh flat-leaf parsley sprigs, optional
Sea salt
Fresh Tomato Sauce, for serving

Stir together the ricotta, basil and black pepper in a small bowl then transfer the mixture to a pastry bag. Remove the stamen from the center of each blossom, then insert the tip of the bag into the center of each blossom and stuff with about 2 tablespoons ricotta. Twist the tips of the petals closed and set aside.

Whisk together the flour and kosher salt in a medium bowl. Add the egg, club soda and olive oil and whisk together to make a batter.

Heat at least 2 inches of canola oil to 375°F in a deep fryer or large saucepan with high sides. Holding it by its stem, gently dip a stuffed blossom into the batter, turning to coat it evenly. Lift the blossom from the batter, letting the excess drip off, and carefully lower it into the hot oil. Fry the blossoms in batches of 4 or 5, spacing them about 1 inch apart and turning once to brown evenly, until golden brown, about 2 minutes.

Using a slotted spoon, transfer the fried blossoms to paper towels to drain.

If making the fried parsley garnish, add the parsley sprigs to the hot oil and fry just until lightly crisped, about 30 seconds. Transfer to the paper towels to drain.

Sprinkle the zucchini blossoms with sea salt, top with the fried parsley, and serve warm with fresh tomato sauce.

FRESH TOMATO SAUCE

Because this sauce is so very simple, it is imperative to use the ripest, most flavorful tomatoes you can get your hands on. This recipe makes enough for 1 pound of spaghetti (or a platter's worth of fried zucchini blossoms).

MAKES ABOUT 4 CUPS

⅓ cup extra-virgin olive oil
20 ripe plum tomatoes (about 4 pounds), peeled, seeded and coarsely chopped

1 teaspoon dried red chili flakes
Kosher salt and freshly ground black pepper
½ cup fresh basil leaves

Heat the oil in a large sauté pan over moderately high heat until quite hot. When the oil is hot, add the tomatoes and red chili flakes. Season lightly with salt and pepper. Cook until the tomatoes are slightly softened, about 5 minutes. Using a potato masher, crush the tomatoes. Continue to cook until the tomatoes are tender and the sauce has thickened, 20 to 25 minutes. Stir in the basil.

If not using right away, the sauce can be stored in refrigerator for up to 3 days.

CASTLE VALLEY MILL SOFT POLENTA

Castle Valley Mill in Doylestown, Pennsylvania, grinds locally grown corn, rye, spelt, hard and soft wheat berries and emmer, also known as farro. Mark Fischer has found an enthusiastic market—Agricola included!—for the small grains that he grinds on refurbished 19th-century mills.

The secret to creamy polenta is patience; you must cook the cornmeal slowly, stirring well and often. You'll know it's ready when the crunchy bite of the ground corn softens.

SERVES 6 TO 8

6 cups Chicken Stock
   (see recipe, page 195)
2 cups stoneground cornmeal
½ cup (1 stick) unsalted butter,
   cut into pieces

Kosher salt and freshly ground
   black pepper
3 tablespoons finely grated
   Parmigiano Reggiano

Bring the stock to a boil in a medium pot over high heat. Whisking constantly, slowly add the cornmeal in a thin stream. Continue whisking until the polenta comes to a simmer, then reduce the heat to low and cook, stirring frequently with a wooden spoon, until the polenta is creamy, about 45 minutes. Remove from the heat and stir in the butter and season with salt and pepper. Stir in the Parmigiano Reggiano and serve.

MASHED RUTABAGAS

Pity the poor misunderstood rutabaga. As a member of the brassica family, it calls the turnip and cabbage kissing cousins and shares some of their crisp, slightly bitter notes. But cooking mellows the rutabaga and brings out its deep sweetness, making it a perfect foil to rich meats like brisket and our Fried Chicken dinner (page 109).

SERVES 4

4 medium rutabagas, peeled and cut into chunks
½ cup whole milk, warmed
½ cup (1 stick) unsalted butter, softened

¼ teaspoon freshly grated nutmeg
Kosher salt and freshly ground black pepper

Cook the rutabagas in a pot of boiling salted water until fork-tender, about 20 minutes. Drain and mash using a large fork. Add the milk, butter and nutmeg and mash until smooth. Season with salt and pepper. Keep warm until ready to serve.

WHIPPED YUKON GOLDS

Josh learned to make these decadent potatoes during his time with chef Thomas Keller in California. Fluffy, rich and super satisfying, they are everything you want in mashed potatoes. Use the best quality cream and butter you can here—it really makes a difference.

SERVES 8 TO 12

6 pounds Yukon gold potatoes, peeled and cut into 2-inch chunks
1 cup (2 sticks) unsalted butter, cut into small cubes

1½ cups heavy cream
Kosher salt and freshly ground white pepper
3 tablespoons minced chives

Put the potatoes in a large pot, cover with cold salted water and bring to a boil.

Simmer the potatoes over moderate heat until tender, about 25 minutes. Drain and return the potatoes to the pot. Cook over moderate heat for 1 minute, shaking the pot to dry the potatoes thoroughly.

Combine the butter and cream in a large saucepan and heat gently over moderately low heat until the butter has melted into the cream. Working over the saucepan, pass the hot potatoes through a ricer or food mill. Stir the potatoes and cream with a wooden spoon until light and fluffy. Season with salt and pepper and stir in the chives.

ROASTED FINGERLING POTATOES WITH ROSEMARY

Their elegant shape and buttery flavor make fingerlings a favorite in our kitchen. They go well with just about anything.

SERVES 4 TO 6

2 tablespoons extra-virgin olive oil

3 pounds fingerling potatoes, halved lengthwise

Sea salt and freshly ground black pepper

2 tablespoons fresh rosemary needles, chopped

Preheat the oven to 375°F. Heat the olive oil in a large ovenproof sauté pan over moderately high heat. Add the potatoes, cut side down, and season with salt and pepper. Cook, undisturbed, until the underside is golden brown, about 8 minutes. Shake the pan to loosen the potatoes and transfer it to the oven. Roast the potatoes for 10 minutes, then sprinkle the rosemary over the potatoes, and continue to roast until tender, 5 to 10 minutes more. Serve immediately.

HANDCUT POTATO FRIES

Though they've been around since the 1940s, when the USDA introduced them, Kennebecs have only recently earned widespread acclaim as chef after chef discovers how deliciously potato-ey they are—especially when fried. In fact, they got their start as a chipping potato, but a meatier cut really lets you taste their nuttiness.

SERVES 4 TO 6

3 pounds Kennebec potatoes

Canola oil, for frying

Kosher salt to taste

Scrub the potatoes and cut lengthwise into ¼-inch-thick sticks. Soak the potatoes in a large bowl of cold water to remove excess starch, then drain well and pat dry with paper towels.

Heat at least 3 inches of oil to 300°F in a deep fryer or large saucepan with high sides. Working in batches, fry the potatoes for 2 minutes then transfer to paper towels to drain and cool.

Increase the oil temperature to 350°F. Working in batches, fry the potatoes a second time until golden brown, 3 to 5 minutes. Drain on paper towels, sprinkle with salt, and serve immediately.

ROASTED CAULIFLOWER

Blasting cauliflower florets in a hot oven concentrates their natural sweetness, turning them into something like vegetable bonbons.

SERVES 4

1 medium head cauliflower (about 2½ pounds), cut into florets

2 tablespoons extra-virgin olive oil
Kosher salt

Preheat the oven to 450°F. Toss the cauliflower florets with the oil and salt to taste in a large bowl. Arrange the florets in 1 layer on a large baking sheet and roast, stirring and turning over occasionally, until tender and golden brown, 25 to 30 minutes.

CARAMELIZED BRUSSELS SPROUTS WITH PANCETTA AND HERBS

Blanching vegetables may seem like a time-consuming extra step, but it really helps preserve their bright color, and makes the finished dish even more appealing. Here, pancetta adds a salty, porky backbone to a dish of sweet, golden-brown Brussels sprouts, though you could certainly do without it.

SERVES 4

1 pound Brussels sprouts, trimmed and halved lengthwise
2 tablespoons extra-virgin olive oil
4 ounces pancetta, diced
1 tablespoon minced shallots
1½ teaspoons chopped fresh thyme leaves

1½ teaspoons chopped fresh sage leaves
Kosher salt and freshly ground black pepper
1 tablespoon chopped fresh chives

Prepare an ice water bath. Cook the Brussels sprouts in a large pot of salted boiling water until tender and bright green, 3 to 4 minutes. Drain, then transfer the sprouts to the ice water bath to cool completely. Drain the cooled sprouts in a colander and dry on kitchen towels.

Heat the olive oil in a large sauté pan over moderate heat. Add the pancetta and cook, stirring occasionally, until golden brown and crisp, 4 to 5 minutes. Using a slotted spoon, transfer the pancetta to a paper towel–lined plate.

Add the Brussels sprouts to the pan and cook over moderate heat, stirring occasionally, until golden brown, about 5 minutes. Return the pancetta to the pan and stir in the shallots, thyme and sage. Cook until heated through, about 1 minute, and season to taste with salt and pepper. Transfer to a serving bowl and garnish with the chives.

DESSERTS

SWEET ENDINGS

With its deep chocolate flavor and whisper of floral heat, this is a cake for grownups. Don't be intimidated by the Italian meringue icing—simultaneously beating the eggs and heating the sugar syrup requires a bit of attention, but if the eggs are ready first, they can sit while the sugar comes to temperature; if the syrup is ready before the eggs, pour it into a glass measuring cup to keep from cooking further. At the restaurant, we use a kitchen torch to burnish the icing's swoops and swirls. If you don't have a torch, you can get a similar effect—on the top only—by running the frosted cake under the broiler for a minute or two.

We get our chocolate from TCHO, a San Francisco-based chocolate maker whose practices are beyond fair trade. Their products are also beyond delicious and well worth seeking out.

To make the cake, preheat the oven to 350°F. Butter three 8-inch round cake pans and line the bottoms with rounds of parchment.

Sift together the flours, baking soda and baking powder in a bowl. Put the butter, brown sugar, vanilla paste, espresso powder and salt in the bowl of a mixer with the paddle attachment and beat until creamy and lightened. Meanwhile, put the cocoa powder in a small bowl and slowly whisk in the egg, egg white and water, whisking until it becomes a completely smooth paste. Slowly add the cocoa paste to the creamed butter mixture, scraping down the sides of the bowl once or twice. Beat in the flour mixture in 3 batches, alternating with the buttermilk, beginning and ending with the flour.

Divide the batter among the 3 pans and smooth the tops. Bake until the center of each cake springs back when touched, 15 to 20 minutes. Cool for 5 minutes in the pans, then turn the cakes out onto a wire cooling rack to cool completely.

While the cakes bake, make the chocolate buttercream filling. Place the chopped chocolates into the bowl of a stand mixer fitted with a whisk attachment. Set aside.

[CONTINUED]

DARK CHOCOLATE CAKE WITH BLACK PEPPER ICING

SERVES 10 TO 12

FOR THE CAKE:

½ cup plus 1 tablespoon all-purpose flour

½ cup plus 1 tablespoon cake flour

¾ teaspoon baking soda

½ teaspoon baking powder

6 tablespoons unsalted butter, softened

1½ cups packed dark brown sugar

1 teaspoon vanilla bean paste

1 tablespoon instant espresso powder

½ teaspoon kosher salt

¾ cup unsweetened cocoa powder, preferably TCHO

1 large egg plus 1 large egg white

½ cup plus 2 tablespoons lukewarm water

½ cup plus 2 tablespoons buttermilk

FOR THE CHOCOLATE BUTTERCREAM FILLING:

8 ounces bittersweet chocolate, preferably TCHO, finely chopped

8 ounces milk chocolate, preferably TCHO, finely chopped

1½ cups heavy cream

2 tablespoons corn syrup

1½ cups (3 sticks) unsalted butter, softened but still cool, cut into 1-inch pieces

FOR THE BLACK PEPPER ICING:

1 cup granulated sugar

¼ teaspoon kosher salt

½ cup water

½ teaspoon freshly ground black pepper

3 large egg whites

Bring the heavy cream and corn syrup to a simmer in a small saucepan. Remove from the heat and pour over the chocolate. Let stand for 2 to 3 minutes then whisk together until the chocolate is completely melted and smooth, and the mixture is thoroughly combined. Let cool to room temperature.

Using the stand mixer, beat the chocolate-cream mixture at medium speed and gradually add the butter, a few pieces at a time, until the butter is thoroughly incorporated and the filling is smooth and silky.

If necessary, trim the top of the three cooled cake layers so they lie flat. Place a cake layer on a serving plate or cake turntable. Spoon half of the buttercream filling onto the cake and smooth it out until you have an even layer spread over the cake. Add the second cake layer and top with the remaining buttercream filling. Top with the final cake layer and then refrigerate until set, about 3 hours. Once the cake has been completely chilled, you can ice it.

To make the icing, set aside 2 tablespoons sugar in a small bowl along with the salt. Put the water, pepper and remaining sugar in a small saucepan. Place the egg whites in a clean bowl of a stand mixer with the whisk attachment. Bring the moistened sugar to a boil over moderately high heat; put a candy thermometer in the syrup.

At the same time you are heating the sugar, begin to whisk the egg whites on medium-high speed. When the egg whites are foamy and lightened, slowly add the reserved sugar and salt and continue to whisk until the whites form firm peaks. Just when your whites are done, your syrup should reach 240°F. Adjust the speed of the mixer or the height of the flame to coordinate the two. When both are done, remove the thermometer from the pot. With the mixer running at medium-high speed, slowly pour the hot syrup down the side of the bowl into the egg whites. Continue to beat the meringue until it has cooled back down to room temperature, 7 to 10 minutes.

Spoon the icing on top of the cake and then smooth it over the sides with an offset spatula to cover the entire cake. Working quickly, make decorative swirls in the icing with your spatula. Use a kitchen torch to lightly caramelize the entire cake.

The first time Josh tried to make this decadent pudding for Agricola restaurateur Jim Nawn's family, their dog Cooper (a chocolate Lab, appropriately enough) ate all the croissants. We don't blame him, but the finished treat is well worth waiting for.

CHOCOLATE CROISSANT BREAD PUDDING

SERVES 8

10 large egg yolks
¾ cup sugar
4 cups heavy cream
2 vanilla beans
6 plain croissants

2 ounces bittersweet chocolate, preferably TCHO, roughly chopped
Vanilla Bean Ice Cream, for serving (page 163)

Preheat the oven to 350°F. Put the egg yolks and sugar in a mixing bowl and whisk until well combined. Pour the cream into a saucepan then split the vanilla beans and scrape the seeds into the pan. Heat the cream over moderately high heat almost to a simmer then slowly pour the hot cream into the egg mixture, whisking constantly until well combined. Set aside, loosely covered, to keep warm.

Cut the croissants into small pieces, arrange on a baking sheet and toast in the oven until golden brown, 8 to 10 minutes. Reduce the heat to 300°F.

Butter a 2-quart gratin dish. Arrange the toasted croissant pieces in the dish and top with the chopped chocolate.

Pour the warm custard mixture over the croissants and chocolate. Place the dish in a roasting pan then fill the roasting pan with enough hot tap water to come halfway up the sides of the soufflé dish. Bake the pudding until firm, 35 to 45 minutes.

Serve warm with vanilla ice cream.

MEYER LEMON CHEESECAKE

SERVES 10 TO 12

FOR THE CHEESECAKE:

5 ounces graham crackers (about 10 full crackers)

1¼ cups plus 3 tablespoons sugar

4 tablespoons unsalted butter, melted

1 tablespoon freshly grated Meyer lemon zest

1 pound cream cheese (two 8-ounce packages), cut into rough chunks and left to stand at room temperature for 30 to 45 minutes

4 large eggs, at room temperature

¼ cup freshly squeezed Meyer lemon juice

2 teaspoons vanilla extract

¼ teaspoon kosher salt

½ cup heavy cream

FOR THE MEYER LEMON CURD:

⅓ cup freshly squeezed Meyer lemon juice

2 large eggs plus 1 large egg yolk

½ cup sugar

2 tablespoons cold unsalted butter, cut into ½-inch cubes

1 tablespoon heavy cream

¼ teaspoon vanilla extract

Pinch of kosher salt

Meyer lemons, in our opinion, are one of Mother Nature's perfect fruits and well worth importing from California during the few winter months they are available. Their taste, while still lemony, is smoother and brighter than a regular lemon, their tartness softened. Meyers are wonderful for baking, and they work beautifully here.

To make the crust, preheat the oven to 325°F. Put the graham crackers in a food processor and process to make fine, even crumbs. Add 3 tablespoons sugar and pulse to combine. Add the melted butter in a slow, steady stream while pulsing; pulse until the mixture is evenly moistened and resembles wet sand.

Transfer the crumb mixture to a 9-inch springform pan; using the bottom of a ramekin or dry measuring cup, press the crumb mixture firmly and evenly into the pan bottom, keeping the sides as clean as possible. Bake until fragrant and golden brown, 15 to 18 minutes. Cool on a wire rack to room temperature, about 30 minutes. When cool, wrap the outside of the pan with two 18-inch-square pieces of heavy-duty foil; set the springform pan in a roasting pan.

While the crust is cooling, make the filling. Process ¼ cup sugar and the lemon zest in the cleaned food processor until sugar is yellow and zest is broken down, about 15 seconds, scraping down bowl if necessary. Transfer the lemon sugar to a small bowl; stir in the remaining 1 cup sugar.

In a standing mixer fitted with a paddle attachment, beat the cream cheese on low speed to soften slightly. With the machine running, add the sugar mixture in a slow, steady stream; increase the speed to medium and continue to beat until the mixture is creamy and smooth, about 3 minutes, scraping down the bowl with a rubber spatula as needed.

Reduce the speed to medium-low and add the eggs 2 at a time; beat until incorporated, about 30 seconds, scraping the sides and bottom of the bowl well after each addition. Add the lemon juice, vanilla and salt and mix until just incorporated. Add the heavy cream and mix until just incorporated. Give the batter a final scrape and stir, and pour into the prepared springform pan.

Fill the roasting pan with enough hot tap water to come

halfway up the sides of the springform pan. Bake the cheesecake until the sides start to puff, the center still jiggles slightly and the surface is no longer shiny. Turn off the oven and prop open the oven door with a wooden spoon handle; let the cake cool in the oven (still in the water bath) for 1 hour.

Transfer the pan to a wire rack; remove the foil and run a small paring knife around the inside edge of the pan to loosen the sides of the cake. Cool the cake to room temperature, about 2 hours.

While the cheesecake bakes, make the Meyer lemon curd. Heat the lemon juice in a small nonreactive saucepan over moderate heat until hot but not boiling. Whisk together the eggs, yolk and sugar in a medium nonreactive bowl. Whisking constantly, slowly pour the hot lemon juice into the eggs, then return the mixture to the saucepan and cook over moderate heat, stirring constantly with a wooden spoon, until it is thick enough to coat a spoon, about 3 minutes.

Immediately remove the pan from the heat and stir in the cold butter until incorporated; stir in the cream, vanilla and salt, then pour the curd through a fine-mesh sieve into a small non-reactive bowl. Cover the surface of the curd directly with plastic wrap; refrigerate until needed.

When the cheesecake is cool, scrape the lemon curd onto the cheesecake (still in the pan). Using an offset spatula, spread the curd evenly over the top of the cheesecake. Cover tightly with plastic wrap and refrigerate for at least 4 hours or up to 24 hours. To serve, remove sides of the pan and cut the cake into wedges.

Roasted sweet potato makes these bite-sized fritters wonderfully moist. Although we serve them after dinner, they would make a great addition to a lavish weekend brunch spread. Grade B maple syrup has a deeper, richer flavor than Grade A.

To make the maple dipping sauce, combine the cream, brown sugar, maple syrup, butter and salt in a heavy saucepan and bring to a boil, stirring occasionally to dissolve the sugar. Remove from the heat and set aside.

To make the beignets, preheat the oven to 375°. Wrap the sweet potato in foil and bake until tender, about 45 minutes. While still warm, peel off the skin. Measure out ¾ cup packed sweet potato flesh.

While the sweet potato bakes, make the cinnamon sugar. Whisk together ½ cup granulated sugar and the cinnamon in a medium bowl and set aside.

Whisk together the flour, baking powder and salt in a medium bowl. In a large bowl, combine the eggs, remaining ½ cup sugar and ¾ cup roasted sweet potato flesh. Add the flour mixture, followed by the milk and melted butter. Mix together with a wooden spoon or a mixer.

Heat at least 3 inches of oil to 325°F in a deep fryer or large saucepan with high sides. Working in batches, carefully drop tablespoons of the batter into the hot oil and fry, flipping halfway through, until golden brown, about 4 minutes. Using a slotted spoon, transfer the beignets to paper towels to drain. Repeat with the remaining batter. Dredge the warm beignets in the cinnamon sugar and serve immediately with warm maple dipping sauce on the side.

SWEET POTATO BEIGNETS WITH MAPLE DIPPING SAUCE

SERVES 6

FOR MAPLE DIPPING SAUCE:

1 cup heavy cream

¾ cup packed dark brown sugar

¼ cup maple syrup, preferably Grade B

4 tablespoons unsalted butter

¼ teaspoon kosher salt

FOR BEIGNETS:

1 large sweet potato

1 cup granulated sugar, divided

1½ teaspoons ground cinnamon

3 cups all-purpose flour

2 teaspoons baking powder

1 teaspoon salt

2 large eggs, lightly beaten

1½ cups whole milk

2 tablespoons unsalted butter, melted

Vegetable oil, for frying

PEACH COBBLER

SERVES 8

8 ripe peaches (about
   3 pounds)
1 cup (2 sticks) plus
   1 tablespoon cold unsalted
   butter, cut into ½-inch
   pieces
1 cup packed light brown sugar
¼ teaspoon vanilla extract
¼ teaspoon ground cinnamon

1¾ cups plus 2 tablespoons
   all-purpose flour, divided
½ cup granulated sugar
2 tablespoons baking powder
1 teaspoon kosher salt
2 large eggs
1 cup whole milk
1½ tablespoons raw sugar

At the restaurant, we serve this summery cobbler in individual skillets, but when we make it at home, we pull out one of our large, well-seasoned cast iron skillets. And what's cobbler without ice cream? We like it best with homemade Brown Sugar Ice Cream (page 163).

Preheat the oven to 350°F. Prepare an ice water bath.

With the tip of a sharp knife, cut a small X in the bottom of each peach. Working in batches, blanch the peaches in a large pot of boiling water for 15 seconds. Transfer the peaches with a slotted spoon to an ice bath to stop the cooking. Peel, pit and slice the peaches.

Melt 1 tablespoon butter in a 12-inch cast iron skillet over moderate heat. Add the sliced peaches, brown sugar, vanilla and cinnamon and cook, stirring occasionally and taking care not to break up the fruit, until the peaches are tender, 8 to 10 minutes. Add 2 tablespoons flour and continue stirring until the filling has thickened slightly. Remove from the heat.

While the filling is cooking, make the cobbler batter. Put the remaining 1¾ cups flour, the granulated sugar, baking powder and salt in an electric mixer with a paddle attachment and mix to combine. Add the remaining 1 cup butter and mix just until small pea-sized pieces of butter remain.

Whisk together the eggs and milk in a small bowl then add to the dry mixture and mix until combined.

Top the hot peach filling with large spoonfuls of cobbler batter; the peaches should be almost completely covered by the batter. Sprinkle the raw sugar all over the batter. Place the skillet on a baking sheet (in case the cobbler bubbles over) and bake until golden brown and a skewer inserted into the top of the cobbler comes out clean, with just a few crumbs attached, 30 to 40 minutes. Serve warm.

When making this freeform, streusel-topped tart, we usually reach for Stayman Winesap apples from nearby Terhune Orchards. Their crisp, sweet-tart flesh makes them an ideal baking apple. We serve wedges of this crostata—warm, of course—with Vanilla Bean Ice Cream (page 163).

Preheat the oven to 375°F. To make the filling, melt the butter in a large heavy pot over moderate heat. Whisk together the apple cider and cornstarch in a bowl to make a slurry. Add the slurry to the melted butter and bring to a boil, whisking constantly, and cook until thickened, about 4 minutes. Add the granulated sugar, cinnamon, nutmeg, allspice and vanilla to the pot. Add the apples and cranberries and cook, stirring occasionally, until the apples are tender, about 10 minutes. Remove from the heat and cool completely.

To make the dough, combine the flour, salt and cold butter in the bowl of a stand mixer with a paddle attachment and mix just until small pea-sized pieces of butter remain in the dough. Add the cold water and vinegar and continue mixing until fully combined; this should only take a few seconds on low speed. Gather the dough into a ball and flatten slightly into a disc. Wrap tightly in plastic wrap and refrigerate for at least 10 minutes before rolling out.

Lightly flour a work surface and roll the dough out into a large circle about ¼-inch thick. Transfer the dough to a parchment lined baking sheet. Spoon the cooled filling over the middle of the dough and gently fold the edges of the dough over the filling, pleating as needed. (Try to keep the filling from leaking out, which will make the crostata soggy.) Refrigerate the assembled crostata while you make the streusel.

To make the streusel, put the brown sugar, oats, flour, butter and salt in a bowl and mix until large chunks of butter remain. Add the sliced almonds and mix briefly to incorporate, taking care not to crumble up the nuts. Sprinkle the streusel over the crostata filling. Lightly beat the egg and brush the border of the pastry with the egg wash. Bake the crostata until the crust is golden brown and the filling is bubbling in the center, 40 to 45 minutes. Let cool at least 15 minutes before cutting into wedges and serving with ice cream.

CRANBERRY APPLE CROSTATA

SERVES 8

FOR THE FILLING:
1 tablespoon unsalted butter
1½ cups apple cider
¼ cup cornstarch
1 cup granulated sugar
1½ teaspoons ground cinnamon
⅛ teaspoon ground nutmeg
Pinch of ground allspice
½ teaspoon vanilla extract
6 medium apples, peeled, cored and thinly sliced
2 cups fresh cranberries

FOR THE DOUGH:
2½ cups all-purpose flour
¼ teaspoon kosher salt
1 cup (2 sticks) cold unsalted butter, cut into cubes
6 tablespoons ice-cold water
2 tablespoons distilled white vinegar

FOR THE OATMEAL ALMOND STREUSEL:
1 cup packed light brown sugar
1 cup rolled oats
½ cup plus 2 tablespoons all-purpose flour
½ cup (1 stick) unsalted butter, softened
½ teaspoon kosher salt
¼ cup sliced almonds
1 large egg

SWEET CORN CAKE WITH LEMON CURD AND BLUEBERRY COMPOTE

This summery cake, crowned with silky lemon curd, gets its pleasingly nubby texture from a bit of cornmeal. It's meant to be served cold on a hot day, so make it in the cool of the morning to be pulled out later as the sun is setting.

SERVES 10 TO 12

FOR THE CAKE:
2 cups cake flour
½ cup semolina flour
½ cup cornmeal
2 teaspoons baking powder
¼ teaspoon kosher salt
1 cup crème fraîche
1 tablespoon vanilla extract
1 cup (2 sticks) plus
    6 tablespoons unsalted
    butter, softened
¾ cup sugar
Finely grated zest of 2 lemons
4 large eggs

FOR THE SYRUP:
¾ cup freshly squeezed
    lemon juice
¾ cup sugar
¼ cup water

FOR THE LEMON CURD:
4 lemons
8 large egg yolks
1 cup sugar
½ cup (1 stick) unsalted butter,
    cut into pieces

FOR THE COMPOTE:
2 cups blueberries
¾ cup sugar
1½ teaspoons freshly squeezed
    lemon juice

Preheat the oven to 325°F. Butter a 10-inch round cake pan, line and line with a round of buttered parchment paper.

Sift together the cake flour, semolina, cornmeal, baking powder and salt in bowl. In a separate small bowl, stir together the crème fraîche and vanilla.

Using a stand mixer, beat together the butter and sugar until fluffy. Add the zest and the eggs one at a time, mixing well and scraping the bowl down after each egg.

Reduce the mixer speed to low and add the flour and crème fraîche mixtures alternately in 3 batches, beginning and ending with the flour mixture and scraping down the bowl after each flour addition. Give the batter a stir by hand to make sure it is evenly mixed.

Pour the batter into the prepared pan. Bake until a wooden skewer inserted into the center of the cake comes out clean, 40 to 50 minutes. Cool the cake in the pan on a rack for 30 minutes, then invert onto the rack to cool.

Make the simple syrup: Combine the lemon juice, sugar and water in a small saucepan. Bring to a boil and cook, stirring, until the sugar has dissolved. Remove from the heat and set aside.

Flip the cake over on the rack, so the top is facing up. Brush some of the lemon syrup over the cake (you will have leftover syrup; store it in the refrigerator for another use).

To make the lemon curd, finely grate the zest of the lemons, then juice enough of the fruit to measure ¾ cup juice. In a medium bowl, whisk together the egg yolks until well combined; set aside.

Combine the lemon juice, zest, sugar and butter in a saucepan over moderately low heat, whisking until the butter is melted and the sugar is dissolved. Add the hot lemon mixture to the yolks in a slow stream, whisking constantly, then pour the mixture back into the saucepan. Continue to cook over moderately low heat, constantly stirring with a wooden spoon in a figure-eight motion, until the curd is thick enough to hold the marks of the spoon, about 5 minutes. Do not boil.

Remove from the heat and strain the curd through a fine-mesh sieve into a bowl set over ice water to cool.

To make the compote, put half the berries in a medium heat-proof bowl. Combine the remaining berries, sugar and lemon juice in a saucepan. Bring to a simmer over moderate heat and cook, stirring, until berries release their juice, about 6 minutes. Increase the heat to high and bring to a boil. Cook, whisking frequently, until thickened, about 2 minutes. Pour over the uncooked berries and fold together with a spatula. Set aside to cool.

To assemble, transfer the cooled cake to a serving plate. Spread with cooled lemon curd and refrigerate. To serve, slice the chilled cake and serve with Blueberry Compote.

Terhune Orchards

Visit Terhune Orchards on a Saturday afternoon in September, and you'll quickly see how popular this farm is. Every year, hundreds of thousands of visitors flock to the 185-acre farm to pick their own apples, shop for cider and juice, and visit the farm animals.

Gary and Pam Mount, the couple behind Terhune Orchards for the last 40 years, started their life together in the late 1960s as volunteers for the newly formed Peace Corps. They lived on the remote islands of Micronesia, Pam teaching and Gary working on agricultural projects. When they returned to the states and took over the orchard in 1975, they hoped to develop the sort of community—a place where everyone works together—that they had experienced in the Peace Corps. Those crowded weekends at the farm attest to their status in the Princeton-area community.

Gary has long been an innovator in the realm of apple propagation. Working on his father's large, conventional apple farm as a young man, he saw the risks of too little diversification and reliance on chemical inputs. From the beginning, he has tested alternatives to pesticides, such as Integrated Pest Management, promoting insects that are beneficial to crop growth and dissuading those that are not. It's a system of strategic intervention that requires constant monitoring, but one that has proved very effective at Terhune Orchards.

ORANGE CARDAMOM ICE CREAM

Though it's easy enough to buy cardamom already ground, the spice loses its potency quickly. Seek out the dried pods, which are usually green or black, and split them open with your fingernail to let loose the small, irregular seeds within. They won't look like much, but as soon as they are ground (an electric spice grinder or mortar and pestle will do the trick), their bracing, spicy fragrance will knock your socks off. Try this ice cream alongside a simple pound cake or our Teff-Almond Cake (page 166).

MAKES ABOUT 1½ QUARTS

2 cups heavy cream
2 cups whole milk
1 cup sugar
1 teaspoon freshly ground
    cardamom
¼ teaspoon kosher salt
1 orange
15 large egg yolks

Combine the cream, milk, ½ cup sugar, cardamom and salt in a heavy saucepan. Finely grate the zest of the orange and juice it (you should have about ¼ cup). Add both the zest and juice to the pan. Heat the mixture over moderate heat, stirring to dissolve the sugar, until it just comes to a gentle simmer.

Meanwhile, whisk together the egg yolks and remaining ½ cup sugar in a bowl. While whisking constantly, slowly pour half of the hot cream mixture into the yolks to temper them. Once incorporated, pour the tempered yolk mixture back into the pan and simmer over moderately low heat, stirring constantly with a wooden spoon, until the custard is thick enough to coat the back of the spoon (do not let boil), 5 to 10 minutes.

Strain the custard through a fine-mesh sieve into a metal bowl set over ice to stop the cooking process. Chill completely.

Freeze the cold custard in an ice cream maker according to the manufacturer's instructions. Transfer the ice cream to a container and freeze for at least 2 hours to firm up.

ORANGE
CARDAMOM

VANILLA BEAN

VANILLA BEAN ICE CREAM

This creamy concoction delivers a wallop of pure vanilla. It's the classic accompaniment to pies, cobblers, cakes, tarts, cookies...you get the picture!

MAKES ABOUT 1½ QUARTS

2 cups heavy cream
2 cups whole milk
1¼ cups sugar
1 vanilla bean
15 large egg yolks

Combine the cream, milk and ¾ cup sugar in a heavy saucepan. Split the vanilla bean lengthwise and scrape the seeds into the cream mixture then drop in the bean, too. Heat the mixture over moderate heat, stirring to dissolve the sugar, until it just comes to a gentle simmer.

Meanwhile, whisk together the egg yolks and the remaining ½ cup sugar. Gradually whisk in about ½ cup of the hot cream mixture to temper the yolks. Once incorporated, pour the tempered yolk mixture back into the pan and simmer over moderately low heat, stirring constantly with a wooden spoon, until the custard is thick enough to coat the back of the spoon (do not let boil), 5 to 10 minutes.

Strain the mixture through a fine-mesh sieve into a metal bowl set over ice to stop the cooking process. Return the vanilla bean to the custard and chill completely.

Discard the vanilla bean and freeze the cold custard in an ice cream maker according to the manufacturer's instructions. Transfer the ice cream to a container and freeze for at least 2 hours to firm up.

BROWN SUGAR ICE CREAM

If white sugar hits a high, clear note, brown sugar goes deeper, darker, richer. Try this ice cream in place of vanilla alongside apple pie or our Peach Cobbler (page 156).

MAKES ABOUT 1½ QUARTS

2 cups heavy cream
2 cups whole milk
½ cup granulated sugar
½ cup light brown sugar
½ teaspoon kosher salt
1 vanilla bean
15 large egg yolks

Put the heavy cream, milk, ¼ cup granulated sugar, ¼ cup brown sugar and salt into a heavy saucepan. Split the vanilla bean lengthwise and scrape the seeds into the pan; add the pod as well. Heat the mixture over moderate heat, stirring to dissolve the sugars, until it just comes to a gentle simmer.

Whisk together the yolks and the remaining sugars. While whisking constantly, slowly pour half of the hot milk mixture into the egg yolks to temper the yolks. Once incorporated, pour the tempered yolk mixture back into the pan and simmer over moderately low heat, stirring constantly with a wooden spoon, until the custard is thick enough to coat the back of the spoon (do not let boil), 5 to 10 minutes.

Strain the mixture through a fine-mesh sieve into a metal bowl set over ice to stop the cooking. Return the vanilla bean to the custard and chill completely.

Discard the vanilla bean and freeze the cold custard in an ice cream maker according to the manufacturer's instructions. Transfer the ice cream to a container and freeze for at least 2 hours to firm up.

BROWN SUGAR

PEACH TARRAGON SORBET

When peaches are at their dripping-down-the-elbow ripest, it's time to break out the ice cream maker.

3 medium ripe peaches (about 1 pound)
1¼ cups water
1 cup sugar
4 sprigs fresh tarragon
1 tablespoon freshly squeezed lemon juice

Prepare an ice water bath. With the tip of a sharp knife, cut a small X in the bottom of each peach. Working in batches, blanch the peaches in a large pot of boiling water for 15 seconds. Transfer the peaches with a slotted spoon to the ice bath to stop the cooking. Peel, pit and slice the peaches, transferring the fruit to a blender as you work. Purée the peaches in the blender until very smooth. You should have about 2 cups peach purée.

Combine the water, sugar, tarragon and lemon juice in a saucepan. Bring to a boil, stirring until the sugar is dissolved, then remove from the heat. Let the syrup sit for 5 minutes to steep. Pluck out and discard the tarragon then let the syrup cool completely. Stir the purée into the cooled syrup and refrigerate until cold.

Freeze the cold mixture in an ice cream maker according to the manufacturer's instructions. Transfer the sorbet to a container and freeze for at least 2 hours to firm up.

ROASTED STRAWBERRY AND THYME SORBET

Roasting early June strawberries concentrates their sweetness, heightens their perfume, and deepens their color. It's a simple step that makes this sorbet a true knockout.

MAKES ABOUT 1 QUART

1 pound fresh strawberries
½ cup confectioners sugar
1 cup granulated sugar
1 cup water
½ cup freshly squeezed lemon juice
4 sprigs fresh thyme

Heat oven to 350°F. Line a baking sheet with parchment paper. Remove the leaves from the strawberries. Gently stir together the whole berries and the confectioners sugar in a bowl, then arrange in a single layer on the lined baking sheet. Roast until the berries turn a shade darker and become juicy, 8 to 10 minutes.

While the strawberries roast, combine the granulated sugar, water, lemon juice, and thyme sprigs in a saucepan and bring to boil over moderately high heat, stirring until sugar is dissolved. Add the roasted strawberries and their juices to the pan and simmer until slightly thickened, 5 to 8 minutes. Remove from the heat.

Remove the thyme sprigs from the pan, strip off any leaves that are still attached, and return the leaves to the pan. Using a hand-held blender, blend the mixture until very smooth. Refrigerate the mixture until very cold, preferably overnight.

Freeze the cold mixture in an ice cream maker according to the manufacturer's instructions. Transfer the sorbet to a container and freeze for at least 2 hours to firm up.

TEFF-ALMOND CAKE WITH RED PLUM COMPOTE

SERVES 12

FOR THE CAKE:

2 cups almond meal

¾ cup teff grain

1½ teaspoons baking powder

1¾ cups (3½ sticks) unsalted
butter, softened

1 cup sugar

3 large eggs

Finely grated zest of 2 lemons

FOR THE PLUM COMPOTE:

2 pounds red plums, pitted and
cut into thick wedges

1 cup sugar, or as needed

2 cinnamon sticks

1 vanilla bean

Orange Cardamom Ice Cream,
for serving

This dense, buttery, gluten-free cake pairs beautifully with the plum compote and our Orange Cardamom Ice Cream (page 162). Josh discovered teff, which has a mild nutty flavor and a fine texture, during his San Francisco years; the grain is the primary ingredient in injera, an Ethiopian flatbread. In Amharic, the words "teff" and "lost" are related, possibly because individual grains of teff are so small that, if dropped on the floor, they would scatter and become impossible to find. In fact, it takes about 150 grains of teff to equal the weight of a single grain of wheat.

To make the cake, preheat the oven to 350°F. Lightly butter a 13 × 9-inch cake pan. Line the bottom of the pan with a round piece of parchment paper and lightly butter the parchment.

Whisk together the almond meal, teff grain and baking powder in a bowl. In another bowl, beat the butter and sugar until light and creamy, either by hand with a wooden spoon or with an electric mixer.

Add the flour mixture and eggs alternately in 4 batches, beginning and ending with the flour mixture and mixing until just combined; do not overbeat. Beat in the lemon zest.

Scrape the mixture into the prepared pan and bake until the edges of the cake begin to pull away from the sides of the pan and a wooden pick inserted in the center of the cake comes out clean, about 1 hour. Let the cake cool in its pan on a wire cooling rack.

To make the compote, combine the plums, 1 cup sugar and the cinnamon sticks in a large saucepan. Using the tip of a sharp knife, split the vanilla bean lengthwise and scrape the seeds into the pan, then add the bean itself. Cook over low heat, stirring often, until the plums are very tender and the compote has thickened, about 45 minutes. Taste the mixture as it cooks and add some of the remaining sugar if the mixture tastes too tart.

Remove the plums from the heat and cool completely. Discard the cinnamon sticks and vanilla bean and transfer the compote to a bowl. Cover and refrigerate until ready to use. (The compote can be made up to 2 days ahead.)

To serve, cut the cake into squares and top with some of the plum compote and a scoop of Orange Cardamom Ice Cream.

Rojo's Roastery

When it came time to design Agricola's coffee program, we knew immediately we wanted to work with David Waldman and Rojo's Roastery. David's intense focus on quality and seasonality is exactly in line with Agricola's philosophy.

A tomato picked on Monday afternoon at Great Road Farm will, ideally, show up on Agricola's menu by Tuesday evening. Coffee beans—which can only grow in the latitudinal bands between the Tropic of Cancer and the Tropic of Capricorn—have a longer journey. Beans grown in Guatemala and picked in February probably won't arrive at Rojo's in Lambertville, New Jersey, until June, due to the time it takes to wash, store and ship them.

Rojo's maintains a direct relationship with its growers in 24 countries, often buying entire lots of the best beans, which are grown at very high elevations without the use of chemical fertilizers. High-elevation beans are smaller, denser and often sweeter and more acidic, a combination that offers greater nuance and flavor complexity. "You can't make a bean better than it is," says David, "but you can certainly make it worse." So it's vitally important to roast the beans for the right amount of time at the proper temperature. It's just as important to properly grind the beans and use excellent quality water. The proof is in the coffee, and Rojo's cups are lively, complex and nuanced—the perfect ending to an Agricola meal.

OUR CHEESEBOARD

For Agricola guests who prefer to end their meal on a less sweet note, we offer a cheeseboard with a selection of local cheeses. The majority of these cheeses come from Valley Shepherd Creamery, in Long Valley, New Jersey, and Cherry Grove Farm, a few miles south of the restaurant, in Lawrenceville.

The completely sustainable Cherry Grove Farm is a 480-acre destination for all things delicious. The milk from their organic, grass-fed cows goes into making award-winning cheeses. The leftover whey feeds their heritage-breed pigs that are free to forage through woodland acreage. In addition, they raise grass-fed lambs and sell beautiful eggs from their chickens, which spend their lives pecking and scratching on the farm's organic pastures.

The Cherry Grove cow's milk cheeses that you'll find most often on our cheeseboard are the Italian Alpine-style Havilah, which develops a unique, granular texture as it ages; the creamy, raw milk Toma; and Rosedale, an Appenzeller-style cheese whose rind is washed in a mixture of apple cider from Terhune Orchards, sassafras root and thyme. The farm also offers cheesemaking classes that are a fantastic introduction to this ancient practice.

Like many of the farmers and producers who provide Agricola with ingredients, Valley Shepherd's Eran Wajswol came to cheesemaking by a circuitous route. He started out studying nuclear engineering but later worked his way into real estate development. Eventually a casual interest in European cheeses and visits to creameries and caves became more serious. He returned to New Jersey where he started raising Dutch Friesian sheep on a 120-acre parcel of land in Long Valley. Over the years Valley Shepherd Creamery has expanded, adding goats and cows in order to prolong the cheesemaking year.

We often have several of Valley Shepherd's cheeses on our cheese plate. Of their sheep's milk cheeses, we most often feature the Manchego-style Shepherd's Basket and the white peppercorn–flecked Pepato. Califon Tome and Crema de Blue are two of their cow's milk offerings that we love, as well as Nettlesome, a creamy, Dutch-style cheese that is threaded through with stinging nettles.

PICKLES, PRESERVES & KITCHEN BASICS

FROM OUR LARDER

PICKLED CARROTS

Delicate champagne vinegar is the perfect acid for pairing with sweet baby carrots.

4 cups water
2½ cups champagne vinegar
½ cup sugar
1 tablespoon kosher salt
2 teaspoons coriander seeds
2 teaspoons fennel seeds

1 teaspoon black peppercorns
1 teaspoon dried red chili
    flakes
3 pounds baby carrots, peeled
    and trimmed

Bring the water, vinegar, sugar and salt to a boil in a saucepan, stirring until the sugar and salt are dissolved. Remove from the heat and cover to keep hot.

Put the coriander seeds, fennel seeds, peppercorns and chili flakes in a small sauté pan and toast, stirring, over moderate heat until fragrant, about 1½ minutes. Remove from the heat and divide evenly between 6 sterilized pint-sized mason jars.

Working in batches, blanch the carrots in a large pot of boiling salted water for 2 minutes. Drain well and pack into the jars. Pour the hot brine over the carrots, stopping ½ inch from the rim of the jar. Run a thin knife between carrots and the side of the jar to eliminate air bubbles. Add more brine if needed. Wipe the rims clean, then screw on the lids and bands until snug but not tight.

Process the jars in a bath of boiling water for 15 minutes (the water should cover the jars by 1 inch; start timing when the water returns to a boil after the jars have been added). Remove the jars from the water and let cool completely, then tighten the lids fully.

QUICK PICKLED ZUCCHINI AND SQUASH

These golden, summer squash pickles are essential to the Agricola Burger (page 113), as well as a frequent component of the Pickled and Fermented Plate, one of the most popular starters on our menu.

1 pound zucchini
1 pound yellow squash
1 large yellow onion, thinly
    sliced
3 tablespoons kosher salt
2 cups cider vinegar

1 cup sugar
1½ teaspoons dry mustard
    powder
1½ teaspoons yellow mustard
    seeds, lightly crushed
1 teaspoon ground turmeric

Cut the zucchini and yellow squash into ⅛-inch-thick slices. Combine the zucchini, squash, onions and salt in a large bowl and toss well to combine. Add 3 cups ice cubes and cold water to cover and stir to make sure all the salt is dissolved. Let stand for 1 hour.

Drain the vegetables well in a colander, making sure to remove any ice that has not melted, and dry them, layered between kitchen towels.

Combine the vinegar, sugar, mustard powder, mustard seeds and turmeric in a saucepan and simmer for 5 minutes. Set aside to cool (if the brine is too hot it will cook the vegetables and make the pickles soft).

Return the vegetables to the cleaned bowl and pour the cool brine over. Stir to combine well then place a plate over the pickles to keep them submerged in the brine. Cover and refrigerate for 24 hours.

Transfer the pickles and brine to 3 pint-size mason jars and seal. These pickles will keep for two weeks, stored in the refrigerator.

PICKLED FENNEL

Try a little of this brine in a Great Dirt Road Martini (page 200). The pickled fennel itself is a delicious garnish for an Agricola Bloody Mary (page 200). It also makes a great snack when enjoyed straight from the jar.

MAKES 4 PINTS

3 cups champagne vinegar
1½ cups water
¾ cup sugar
4 teaspoons kosher salt
2 teaspoons coriander seeds
2 teaspoons fennel seeds

½ teaspoon dried red chili flakes
4 medium fennel bulbs (3 to 3½ pounds total), trimmed, cored and cut lengthwise into ¼-thick slices

Bring the vinegar, water, sugar and salt to a boil in a saucepan, stirring until the sugar and salt are dissolved. Remove from the heat and cover to keep hot.

Put the coriander seeds, fennel seeds and chili flakes in a small sauté pan and toast, stirring, over moderate heat until fragrant, about 1½ minutes.

Divide the spices evenly between 4 sterilized pint-sized mason jars. Pack the jars with the raw fennel. Pour the hot brine over the fennel, stopping ½ inch from the rim of the jar. Run a thin knife between the fennel and the sides of the jar to eliminate air bubbles. Add more brine if needed. Wipe the rims clean, then screw on the lids and bands until snug but not tight.

Process the jars in a bath of boiling water for 15 minutes (the water should cover the jars by 1 inch; start timing when the water returns to a boil after the jars have been added). Remove the jars from the water and let cool completely, then tighten the lids fully.

PICKLED CELERY ROOT

This shredded, snowy-white pickle adds a bracing note to a rich charcuterie plate.

MAKES 4 PINTS

4 large celery roots (about 5 pounds total), trimmed and peeled
2¾ cups champagne vinegar
2¾ cups water
3 tablespoons honey
Finely grated zest of 1 lemon

1 tablespoon freshly squeezed lemon juice
1 tablespoon sugar
1 tablespoon kosher salt
2 teaspoons black peppercorns
12 fresh thyme sprigs
4 bay leaves

Using a box grater, grate the peeled celery root; you should have about 16 cups. Combine the vinegar, water, honey, lemon zest, lemon juice, sugar, salt and grated celery root in a large saucepan, cover, and bring to a boil. Set a colander over a large bowl, then drain the celery root in the colander, reserving the brine. Cover tightly to keep hot.

Divide the peppercorns, thyme sprigs and bay leaves evenly among 4 sterilized pint jars.

Pack the jars with the celery root, then top with the hot brine, stopping ½ inch from the rim of the jar. Run a thin knife between the celery root and the side of the jar to eliminate air bubbles. Add more brine if needed. Wipe the rims clean, then screw on the lids and bands until snug but not tight.

Process the jars in a bath of boiling water for 15 minutes (the water should cover the jars by 1 inch; start timing when the water returns to a boil after the jars have been added). Remove the jars from the water and let cool completely, then tighten the lids fully.

PICKLED RED BEETS

This is one of our very favorite pickles. The brine is deeply flavored with red wine and brown sugar.

MAKES 3 PINTS

2 pounds red beets
2 tablespoons extra-virgin
   olive oil
Kosher salt
16 fresh thyme sprigs
2 cups red wine vinegar
1 cup red wine
½ cup water
⅓ cup packed light brown
   sugar
¼ cup honey
1 tablespoon black peppercorns

Preheat the oven to 400°F. Toss the beets with the oil and season with salt. Divide the beets and 10 thyme sprigs between 2 large squares of aluminum foil. Fold up the foil to form pouches and roast until the beets are tender, 45 minutes to 1 hour. Once the beets are cool enough to handle, rub the skins off with a paper towel. Slice the beets into ¼-inch-thick wedges.

Bring the vinegar, wine, water, brown sugar, honey and 1 tablespoon salt to a boil, stirring until the sugar and salt are dissolved. Remove from the heat and cover to keep hot.

Divide the peppercorns and remaining 6 thyme sprigs among 3 sterilized pint-sized mason jars. Pack the beets into the jars. Pour the hot brine over the beets, stopping ½ inch from the rim of the jar. Run a thin knife between beets and the side of the jar to eliminate air bubbles. Add more brine if needed. Wipe the rims clean, then screw on the lids and bands until snug but not tight.

Process the jars in a bath of boiling water for 15 minutes (the water should cover the jars by 1 inch; start timing when the water returns to a boil after the jars have been added). Remove the jars from the water and let cool completely, then tighten the lids fully.

FROM THE FARMER
Beets: Colorful and Versatile

Golden, red and ruby-striped Chioggia beets are staples of both Great Road Farm and Agricola. They grow well in our soil, and Josh absolutely loves them. We like to harvest the beets when they're small, so all they need is a quick scrub to get the dirt off. Then we crank up the oven and roast them whole. They show up all over the menu—pickled, as an accompaniment to the popular Goat Cheese and Potato Terrine, even in our ketchup. Beets keep longer in the fridge when you lop off the greens first, but don't toss those glossy leaves! Washed well, the greens can be eaten raw as an earthy salad or sautéed with onions or garlic and olive oil for a quick side dish.

FROM THE FARMER
Radishes: The Raw and the Cooked

Everyone should try planting radishes in their garden—they grow quickly, require little maintenance and reward you with a beautiful harvest. Deep green leaves and alabaster shoulders give way to pink, cherry-red, purple or pale green bulbs—indeed, pulling radishes from the dirt can feel like you are uncovering a work of art. A bite of their crisp, colorful flesh reveals flavors running the gamut from sweet and mild to eye-tingling and peppery. White-tipped French Breakfast and elegant, slender Shun-kyo radishes are stunning in raw salads or served simply with a smear of butter and a sprinkling of sea salt. Radishes are also delicious sautéed, and they pickle well, tinting their brine a rosy pink. Storage radishes such as the Watermelon and Black Radish keep for up to three months after harvest, which allows us to extend our season during the winter and provides a splash of color on our winter salads. At the farm, we are also experimenting with growing daikon, which will go into our jars of kimchi.

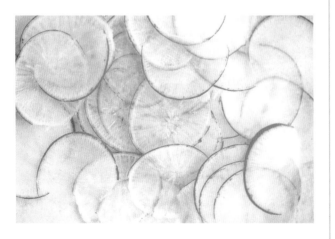

PICKLED RADISHES

These pickles are very pretty in pink, with a little kick, depending on how hot the radishes you use are.

MAKES 3 PINTS

1 tablespoon black peppercorns
2 teaspoons coriander seeds
2 teaspoons fennel seeds
2 cups water
1½ cups distilled white vinegar
3 tablespoons kosher salt
1 tablespoon sugar
2 pounds radishes, trimmed and left whole if bite-sized or halved lengthwise if larger
6 fresh thyme sprigs

Put the peppercorns, coriander seeds and fennel seeds in a small sauté pan and toast, stirring, over moderate heat until fragrant, about 1½ minutes. Remove from the heat and transfer to a small plate to cool.

Bring the water, vinegar, salt and sugar to a boil in a saucepan, stirring until the salt and sugar are dissolved. Remove from the heat and cover to keep hot.

Pack the radishes and thyme sprigs into 3 sterilized pint-sized mason jars, and divide the toasted spices evenly between the jars. Pour the hot brine over the radishes, stopping ½ inch from the rim of the jar. Run a thin knife between radishes and the side of the jars to eliminate air bubbles. Add more brine if needed. Wipe the rims clean, then screw on the lids and bands until snug but not tight.

Process the jars in a bath of boiling water for 15 minutes (the water should cover the jars by 1 inch; start timing when the water returns to a boil after the jars have been added). Remove the jars from the water and let cool completely, then tighten the lids fully.

Variation: We use this same recipe to make Pickled Pearl Onions. To do so, simply substitute 2 pounds peeled pearl onions for the radishes.

PICKLED PUMPKIN

In the fall and winter, you'll find cubes of these sweet-tart pickles dotting our Famous Kale Salad (page 53). They would also taste great served with a wedge of creamy cheese, some crusty bread and a pint of hard cider.

MAKES 4 PINTS

4 pounds sugar pumpkin
  or butternut squash
3 cups apple cider vinegar
2 cups water
2 cups granulated sugar

20 black peppercorns
15 whole cloves
10 allspice berries
2 cinnamon sticks, crushed
1 bay leaf

Peel and seed the pumpkin and cut into ⅓-inch cubes; you should have about 8 cups.

Put the vinegar, water and sugar in a large pot and bring to a simmer over moderate heat, stirring until the sugar is dissolved.

Place the peppercorns, cloves, allspice, cinnamon sticks and bay leaf in a muslin spice bag or tie them tightly in a square of cheesecloth. Add the pumpkin cubes and spice bag to the vinegar mixture. Bring to a boil then reduce the heat to moderately low and simmer the pumpkin until the chunks are translucent and can be easily pierced with a fork, 30 to 45 minutes. Discard the spice bag.

Divide the pumpkin and brine evenly among 4 pint-sized sterilized mason jars, stopping ½ inch from the rim of the jar. Run a thin knife between the pumpkin and the side of the jar to eliminate air bubbles. Add more brine if needed. Wipe the rims clean, then screw on the lids and bands until snug but not tight.

Process the jars in a bath of boiling water for 15 minutes (the water should cover the jars by 1 inch; start timing when the water returns to a boil after the jars have been added). Remove the jars from the water and let cool completely, then tighten the lids fully.

WATERMELON RIND PICKLE

A real Southern specialty, these sweet and tangy pickles would be right at home at a cookout alongside barbecued ribs, burgers and grilled sausages.

MAKES 2 PINTS

One 5-pound piece water-
  melon, quartered
3 tablespoons kosher salt
2 cups sugar
1¼ cups apple cider vinegar
8 dried cloves

8 black peppercorns
2 cinnamon sticks
½ teaspoon pickling spice
¼ teaspoon ground allspice
¼ teaspoon ground ginger

Cut the watermelon pulp from the rind, leaving a thin layer of pink on the rind (reserve the pulp for another use). Cut away and discard the green outer skin from the rind. Cut enough of the rind into ½-inch pieces to measure 4 cups.

Combine 8 cups water and 2 tablespoons salt in a large pot and bring to a boil. Add the rind pieces and boil until tender, 3 to 5 minutes. Drain well and transfer the rinds to a large bowl.

Combine the sugar, vinegar, cloves, peppercorns, cinnamon sticks, pickling spice, allspice, ginger and remaining 1 table-spoon salt in a saucepan. Bring to a boil, stirring until the sugar dissolves. Pour the hot brine over the watermelon rinds. Place a plate on top of the rinds to submerge them in the brine. Cover and refrigerate for at least 8 hours or overnight.

The following day, set a colander over a saucepan, and add the rinds and brine to the colander to drain. Bring the strained brine to a boil. Put the rinds and spices into a cleaned bowl and pour the hot liquid over the rinds. Cover and refrigerate over-night. Repeat this process—straining the brine, boiling it and pouring it over the rinds—one more time. Let cool completely then transfer the rinds and brine to an airtight container and refrigerate.

The pickled watermelon keeps, refrigerated, for several weeks.

What We Think About
When We Think About Pickles

START SMALL: At Agricola, we have the personnel and space to put up dozens of pints of pickles at a time, but at home, canning and preserving is far less daunting when you work in small batches. Choosing to make four jars of pickled beets is much more do-able than tackling an entire bushel's worth. Most of the recipes in this chapter yield a tidy amount and require just an hour or two in the kitchen.

START FRESH: Always work with the ripest, most flavorful produce you can find. The idea of canning is to preserve something at its bright and tasty best to enjoy when the weather is bleak and the ground is hard.

START CLEAN: Sterilization is one of the most important steps in preserving, but also the most stressful for many people. Really, it's quite simple, especially when working in small batches. Start by washing the jars, lids and screw bands in hot, soapy water and rinsing them well, then put the empty jars on a rack in a canning pot (the same one you will use for processing). Fill the pot with water, covering the jars by a couple of inches, put the lid on and bring the water to a boil. Boil the jars for 10 minutes. Turn off the heat and keep the jars submerged in the hot water, with the pot lid on, until you are ready to use them. Meanwhile, heat the lids in water in a small pan until hot (temperature should measure 180°F on an instant-read thermometer); then remove from the heat and keep covered until ready to use.

TURN UP THE HEAT: Toasting the spices before adding them to the jars will add an extra dimension of flavor to your finished pickles. This step, which takes just a minute or two, really encourages the flavors of the spices to bloom.

LIKE LIKES LIKE: When pairing vegetables with vinegars, think about colors and flavors. A red wine vinegar pairs well with a dark red beet, but would discolor more delicate fennel or celery root. Champagne or white wine vinegar would be a better choice in that case.

THINK LIKE A SARDINE: Do your best to really pack those vegetables into the jars, which helps keep them submerged in the brine. If you don't have enough to fully fill a final jar, simply cover the remaining vegetables with brine, refrigerate, and eat sooner rather than later.

LISTEN FOR THE PING: Most pickles require 15 minutes of active boiling to process and seal—start timing when the water comes back to a boil after the jars have gone in. When time's up, carefully remove the jars and set them aside (at least an inch away from each other) to cool. As the jars cool, each should make a *ping* and the lids should become slightly concave. Concave is key—it shows that the vacuum seal was made. Any lids that don't show this seal should be transferred to the fridge and eaten first.

AND THEN, ENJOY: Gazing at a shelf lined with jars of homemade pickles is almost enjoyment enough, but eating them is even more satisfying. One last tip: When pulling pickles from a jar for our Pickled and Fermented Plate, we always let them drain well before plating them. That way, your first bite tastes of the pickled vegetable itself, not just the brine it's been sitting in.

RED BEET KETCHUP

Beets grow extremely well at Great Road Farm, and we are always looking for different ways to showcase them. Josh came up with this bright and zesty combination, and our Handcut Potato Fries (page 141) have never been the same.

MAKES ABOUT 1 PINT

1½ pounds red beets
1 tablespoon extra-virgin olive oil
1 medium yellow onion, finely chopped
3 garlic cloves, minced
2 cups red wine vinegar
1 cup sugar
Kosher salt and freshly ground black pepper

Preheat oven to 400°F. Scrub the beets to clean off any dirt, cutting any extra large beets in half. Arrange the beets on a large piece of aluminum foil, drizzle with the olive oil and wrap tightly to form a pouch. Roast the beets until very tender and easily pierced with the tip of a paring knife, 1 to 1½ hours, depending on the size of the beets. When cool enough to handle, peel and chop the beets; you should have about 3 cups.

Combine the beets, onions, garlic, vinegar and sugar in a large pot. Bring to a boil, then reduce the heat to moderately low and simmer, stirring occasionally, until the mixture is reduced and a deeper color, 45 minutes to 1 hour. Season assertively with salt and pepper.

Working in batches, use a blender and purée until very smooth. Cool completely, then taste again and adjust the seasoning. Transfer the ketchup to an airtight container. Stored in the refrigerator, the ketchup will keep up to 1 month.

CRANBERRY AIGRE-DOUX

Our cranberries come from Paradise Hill Farm, a family-owned farm located in New Jersey's Pine Barrens. Their 200 acres of cranberry bogs keep us well-stocked, and we love to preserve the fruit at its peak. We pickle the cranberries, and also use them to create this interesting sweet and sour combination, which pairs well with rich dishes like Chicken Liver Mousse (page 29). Or try it in place of the usual cranberry relish at Thanksgiving.

MAKES 4 PINTS

2 cups red wine
¾ cup red wine vinegar
¾ cup honey
2 teaspoons kosher salt
2 vanilla beans
2 teaspoons black peppercorns
4 star anise pods
1½ pounds cranberries, well rinsed

Combine the wine, vinegar, honey and salt in a saucepan. Split the vanilla beans lengthwise, scrape the seeds into the pot then add the beans as well. Bring to a boil.

Divide the peppercorns and star anise pods evenly between 4 sterilized pint-sized mason jars. Use tongs to pull out the vanilla beans and put one half of a bean in each jar.

Pack the jars with the cranberries. Pour the hot brine over the cranberries, stopping ½ inch from the rim of the jar. Run a thin knife between the cranberries and the side of the jar to eliminate air bubbles. Add more brine if needed. Wipe the rims clean, then screw on the lids and bands until snug but not tight.

Process the jars in a bath of boiling water for 15 minutes (the water should cover the jars by 1 inch; start timing when the water returns to a boil after the jars have been added). Remove the jars from the water and let cool completely, then tighten the lids fully.

In the last several years preserved lemons—whole lemons that have been packed with salt and lemon juice and left to ferment until the skins become soft and supple—have skipped from Moroccan home kitchens squarely into the mainstream. One whiff of the tart brininess they add to stews, pastas and salads and you'll be converted. Making preserved lemons is a simple art to master and a great introduction to fermenting food at home. Most recipes that call for preserved lemon use only the rind; the pulp is discarded.

Pour 2 cups lemon juice into a clean 2-quart glass jar then add 1 tablespoon sea salt and bay leaves and, the remaining spices.

Using a sharp knife, make 5 lengthwise slits in each lemon, leaving ½ inch intact at both ends. Squeeze open each slit and use your fingers to add a generous amount of sea salt to each opening. Gently reshape the fruit when you are done. After you salt each lemon, pack it into the jar, pressing on it to release its juices and to make room for the remaining lemons. Depending on the size of the lemons and how well you pack them in, you should be able to fit 8 to 10 lemons.

Add the remaining ½ cup lemon juice and any remaining salt to the jar. Cover the lemons the rest of the way with water, leaving some air space at the top, then seal with a lid. Let the lemons ripen for at least 30 days at room temperature, shaking the jar a couple times a week to distribute the salt and spices.

The preserved lemons can be kept at room temperature or refrigerated.

PRESERVED LEMONS

MAKES 8 TO 10 PRESERVED LEMONS

2 to 2½ cups freshly squeezed lemon juice (from 8 to 12 lemons)
½ cup fine sea salt
2 bay leaves
2 tablespoons coriander seeds

7 whole cloves
5 black peppercorns
1 cinnamon stick
8 to 10 unwaxed lemons (preferably Meyer lemons)

BEET AND CABBAGE SAUERKRAUT

Beets add a touch of sweetness to sauerkraut, one of the classic lacto-fermented dishes of the world. The various lactic acid bacteria that perform the fermentation are naturally present on the finely shredded cabbage so there is no need to add any bacteria or starter. Given the right conditions, it will simply "do its thing." Studies have proven that fermented cabbage is incredibly good for you, and though the scientific process behind fermentation sounds complicated, it's actually very easy to do. If you want to learn more about fermenting, Sandor Katz's book *Wild Fermentation* (Chelsea Green, 2003) is a good place to start. It's an interesting, easy-to-understand primer on this ancient practice.

Note that it's vital to use a wide-mouth jar for this recipe, so that you can fit a smaller jar on top, which will weigh down the vegetables and keep them submerged in the brine. If you get really into fermenting, it's worth investing in a pickling crock so you can make larger batches.

MAKES ABOUT 1 QUART

1 medium green cabbage, finely chopped (1½ to 2 pounds)
2 medium beets, peeled and grated

2 garlic cloves, finely chopped
1 tablespoon kosher salt, plus more if needed to make brine
2 teaspoons caraway seeds

Put the cabbage and beets into a large bowl. Add the garlic, 1 tablespoon salt and caraway seeds.

Using your hands, mix everything together thoroughly, scrunching the cabbage to help release its juices. Continue mixing and scrunching for a few minutes. If you tilt the bowl and move the cabbage out of the way, you should see juice starting to collect in the bottom of the bowl. Set the mixture aside and let it sit for about 30 minutes to soften.

Tightly pack the cabbage mixture into a clean 1-quart wide-mouth glass jar, tamping it down to remove as many air pockets as possible.

If the juice does not fully cover the vegetables, add some brine. For 1 cup brine, stir together 1 teaspoon salt and 1 cup filtered water until the salt is dissolved. Pour enough brine into the jar so that vegetables are submerged. Set a small glass jar (filled with water and sealed) on top of the vegetables to help submerge them in the brine. Loosely cover the jar with cheesecloth. Set the jar aside in a cool room temperature place for 1 week.

After 1 week, check to make sure that the sauerkraut has a crisp, tangy smell, the brine level has risen as the salt continues to pull water out of the vegetables, and the color has deepened as the beet juice permeates the cabbage. Put the weight back on top and store again.

Over a couple of weeks, the sauerkraut's flavor will mature and become more complex—less salty, more tangy, with the flavor of the beet really shining through. Taste it every few days and when it is to your liking, seal the jar and transfer it to the refrigerator.

During Agricola's first year, Steve grew 400 pounds of napa cabbage at Great Road Farm, and sous chef Peter Maglaty turned it into beautiful kimchi. In Korea, family kimchi recipes are as personal as fingerprints and thousands of variations exist. It is most often served as one of many side dishes, collectively known as banchan, as part of a meal. At the restaurant, we use it as a seasoning for dishes like Brussels sprouts and our Kimchi Fried Rice (page 95).

NAPA CABBAGE AND DAIKON KIMCHI

MAKES ABOUT 1 QUART

2 pounds napa cabbage (about 1 large head)
¼ cup kosher salt
5 garlic cloves, finely grated
1 teaspoon finely grated fresh ginger
1 teaspoon sugar

1 to 5 tablespoons *gochugaru* (Korean red chili flakes)
8 ounces daikon, peeled and julienned
4 scallions, trimmed and cut into 1-inch pieces

Cut the cabbage lengthwise into quarters and remove the cores. Cut each quarter crosswise into 2-inch-wide strips.

Place the cabbage and salt in a large bowl. Start scrunching the cabbage with your hands until it starts to soften a bit. Put a plate on top and weigh it down with something heavy, like a jar or can of beans. Let stand for 2 hours.

Rinse the cabbage under cold water very well and drain in a colander.

Meanwhile, combine the garlic, ginger and sugar in a small bowl. Mix in the Korean red chili flakes, using 1 tablespoon for a mild blend and up to 5 tablespoons for a very spicy one (we like to use about 3½ tablespoons).

Gently squeeze as much remaining water from the cabbage as possible and return it to the cleaned bowl. Add the daikon, scallions and chili paste. Mix thoroughly using your hands (it is best to wear disposable gloves to protect yourself from the chili flakes). Gently work the paste into the vegetables until they are thoroughly coated. Tightly pack the kimchi into a clean 1-quart wide-mouth glass jar, pressing down on the mixture until the brine rises to cover the vegetables. Set a small glass jar (filled with water and sealed) on top of the vegetables to help submerge them in the brine.

Loosely cover the jar with cheesecloth and set aside at cool room temperature for 3 days. You may see bubbles inside the jar, and brine may seep out of the lid; place a bowl or plate under the jar to catch any overflow. Check the kimchi once a day, pressing down on the vegetables with a spoon to keep them submerged under the brine.

After 3 days, taste the kimchi. If it tastes ripe enough for your liking, seal the jar and transfer it to the refrigerator. You may eat it right away, but it's best after another two weeks.

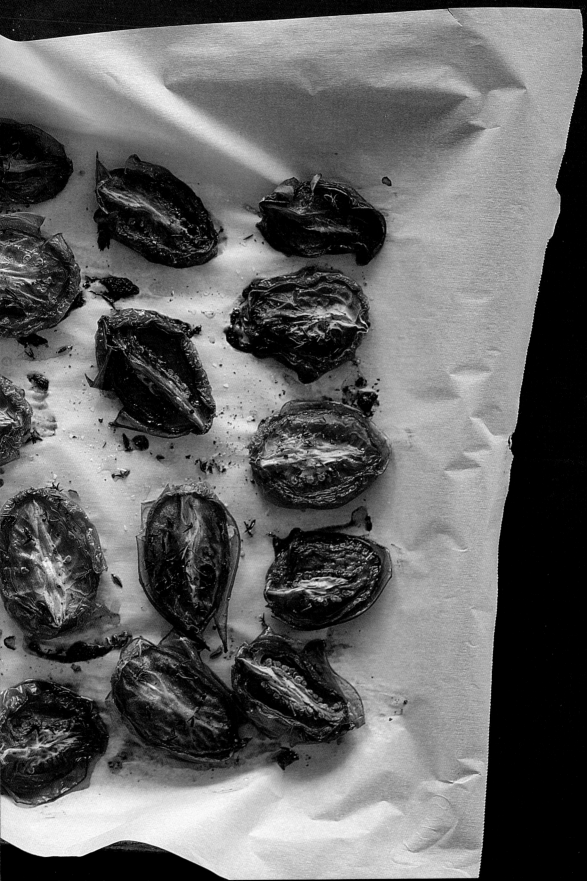

DILLY BEANS

Lacto-fermenting gives dilly beans their signature tang while preserving their enzymes and vitamins. When fermenting foods, it's a good idea to drape cheesecloth over the jar to keep any bugs from getting in. If you see any mold beginning to grow on top of the brine, simply scrape it off. As long as the vegetables are submerged under the brine and not exposed to air, they are fine.

MAKES 2 QUARTS

3 tablespoons kosher salt
4 cups room temperature water
6 fresh dill sprigs, including
    flowering heads if possible
4 garlic cloves, peeled and
    smashed

2 tablespoons dried red chili
    flakes
1 teaspoon black peppercorns
1 pound green beans, trimmed

Stir the salt into the 4 cups water until dissolved. Set aside.

Divide the dill, garlic, red chili flakes and peppercorns evenly between 2 quart jars. Tightly pack the beans into the jars (straight up if the beans are long and thin or sideways if thicker and cut into chunks). Fill the jars with the brine solution, stopping 1 inch from the top of the jar. Set a small glass jar (filled with water and sealed) on top of the beans to help submerge them in the brine.

Loosely cover the jars with cheesecloth and set aside in a cool room temperature place for 7 to 10 days. After 7 days, taste a bean. If it tastes ripe enough for your liking, seal the jars and transfer them to the refrigerator, or continue to let the beans ferment for a few days longer until they suit your taste (they will get tangier the longer they ferment).

OVEN-DRIED TOMATOES

We preserve summer's tomato bounty by making sauce, of course, but we also put up jars of these slow-roasted tomatoes, preserved in olive oil. They add a vibrant pop of flavor to salads, cheese boards and antipasto plates.

MAKES ABOUT 2 CUPS

3 pounds ripe roma tomatoes
    (about 15 tomatoes)
¼ cup extra-virgin olive oil,
    plus more for covering

Leaves from 1 large bunch
    fresh thyme
Kosher salt and freshly ground
    black pepper

Preheat the oven to 250°F. Line a baking sheet with parchment paper.

Cut each tomato in half lengthwise and arrange, cut sides up, on the baking sheet. Drizzle the olive oil over the tomatoes and scatter the thyme leaves over top. Season with salt and pepper.

Bake the tomatoes until they're shriveled and almost dried, but still have a little juice inside, about 4 hours. Let cool, then serve or pack the tomatoes in a mason jar and cover with extra-virgin olive oil, seal and store in the refrigerator. Return to room temperature before serving.

VEGETABLE STOCK

Vegetable stock is a workhorse in our kitchen. Using it in place of water greatly improves the flavor of many of our vegetable- and meat-based dishes. This stock loses its flavor quickly, so make it and use it.

MAKES ABOUT 4 QUARTS

2 large onions, coarsely chopped
1 pound carrots, coarsely chopped
1 bunch leeks, white part only, coarsely chopped
1 bunch celery, coarsely chopped
1 fennel bulb, coarsely chopped
½ bunch flat-leaf parsley, coarsely chopped
¼ cup vegetable oil
6 fresh thyme sprigs
3 bay leaves
4 quarts water

Working in batches if necessary, put the onions, carrots, leeks, celery, fennel and parsley in a food processor and pulse until they are finely chopped. (Processing the vegetables this way will extract the maximum amount of flavor.)

Heat the oil in a medium stockpot over moderately high heat. Add the vegetable mixture, thyme and bay leaves and cook, stirring occasionally, until the vegetables are softened, about 8 minutes. Cover with the water and bring to a boil. Reduce the heat and simmer, skimming frequently, for 1 hour.

Strain through a fine-mesh sieve and cool completely. The stock may be refrigerated, tightly covered, for 4 days or frozen for 1 month.

MUSHROOM STOCK

Although a mixture of mushrooms will produce a more complex flavor, regular white button mushrooms work perfectly for this stock. It is essential to our Mushroom Soup with Roasted Cipollini Onions (page 12).

MAKES ABOUT 4 QUARTS

4 pounds mushrooms, trimmed and sliced
1 large carrot, coarsely chopped
1 medium onion, coarsely chopped
1 medium leek, coarsely chopped
½ bunch flat-leaf parsley, coarsely chopped
6 fresh thyme sprigs
2 tablespoons unsalted butter
¼ teaspoon curry powder
3 bay leaves
1 tablespoon black peppercorns
6 quarts water

Working in batches if necessary, put the mushrooms, carrots, onions, leeks, parsley and thyme in a food processor and pulse until finely chopped.

Heat the butter in a large stockpot over moderate heat, add the curry powder and the vegetable mixture and cook, stirring occasionally, until the vegetables are tender, about 15 minutes. Add the bay leaves and peppercorns and cover with the water. Bring to a boil then reduce the heat and simmer until reduced to about 4 quarts, about 1½ hours.

Strain the stock through a fine-mesh sieve and cool completely. The stock may be refrigerated, tightly covered, for up to 4 days or frozen for up to 1 month.

CHICKEN STOCK

We love the flavor and body that chicken feet add to stock. Adding ice to the pot when the stock just reaches a simmer is an efficient way to remove many of the impurities that are normally removed by skimming with a spoon.

MAKES ABOUT 4 QUARTS

4 pounds chicken backs and necks

3 pounds chicken feet

6 quarts cold water

6 cups ice cubes

2 celery ribs, coarsely chopped

1 large carrot, coarsely chopped

1 large yellow onion, coarsely chopped

10 flat-leaf parsley sprigs and stems

8 fresh thyme sprigs

1 bay leaf

2 teaspoons black peppercorns

Rinse the chicken parts well under cold running water for 5 minutes then place in a large stockpot along with the water. Bring to a simmer over moderate heat, top with the ice and skim off any impurities and fats that rise and stick to the ice. After the stock is skimmed, add the celery, carrots, onions, parsley, thyme, bay leaf and peppercorns to the pot. Return to a simmer and cook, skimming occasionally, until the stock is golden and reduced to about 4 quarts, 2½ to 3 hours.

Strain the stock through a fine-mesh sieve and let cool completely. The stock can be refrigerated, tightly covered, for up to 4 days, or frozen for months.

BEEF STOCK

Roasting the beef and its bones until deeply caramelized is what gives this stock its remarkable depth of flavor.

MAKES ABOUT 4 QUARTS

4 tablespoons vegetable oil

3 pounds beef shanks or bone-in chuck steaks (cut up by your butcher)

8 white mushrooms, coarsely chopped

2 large carrots, coarsely chopped

2 celery ribs, coarsely chopped

1 large yellow onion, unpeeled and coarsely chopped

1 head garlic, halved crosswise

1 tablespoon tomato paste

10 flat-leaf parsley sprigs and stems

8 fresh thyme sprigs

2 bay leaves

1 teaspoon black peppercorns

5 quarts water

6 cups ice cubes

Put a roasting pan in the oven and preheat the oven to 450°F. Add 2 tablespoons vegetable oil to the hot roasting pan. Add the meat and bones in a single layer and roast, flipping occasionally, until golden brown on all sides, about 45 minutes. Set aside.

Heat the remaining 2 tablespoons oil in a large stockpot over moderately high heat. Add the mushrooms, carrots, celery, onions and garlic and cook, stirring occasionally, until deep golden brown and softened, about 15 minutes. Add the tomato paste and cook for 2 minutes, stirring once or twice to evenly distribute it. Add the parsley, thyme, bay leaves and peppercorns and a few cups of the water, stirring and scraping the bottom of the pot with a wooden spoon to loosen any browned bits. Add the reserved meat and bones and remaining water to the pot. Bring to a boil then reduce the heat to low and simmer gently until reduced to about 4 quarts, 4 to 5 hours, skimming the surface of the stock from time to time and adding more water if necessary to keep the bones covered.

Top the hot stock with ice and skim off any impurities and fats that rise and stick to the ice. Strain through a fine-mesh sieve and cool completely. The stock can be refrigerated, tightly covered, for up to 4 days, or frozen for months.

DRINKS

RAISE A GLASS

GREAT DIRT ROAD MARTINI

A dirty martini, farm-style. Using the brine from homemade pickles is what gives this drink its singular verve, so choose your favorite. Just remember that brine from, say, pickled radishes will tint your drink pink, while that from pickled fennel, pearl onions or celery root will keep things clear.

MAKES 1 DRINK

2 ounces (¼ cup) vodka, preferably Crop Organic

½ ounce (1 tablespoon) dry vermouth, preferably Vya

½ ounce (1 tablespoon) pickling brine

1 piece pickled vegetable, skewered

Fill a stirring glass with ice. Add the vodka, vermouth and pickling brine to the glass. Stir briskly for 15 seconds then strain into a chilled martini glass. Garnish with the skewered pickled vegetable.

AGRICOLA BLOODY MARY

Walking through the restaurant during brunch, you'll see at least one of these on almost every table. Freshly grated horseradish and hot sauce make this as good a wake-up call as any cup of joe.

MAKES 1 DRINK

5 ounces (about ⅔ cup) tomato juice (not from concentrate)

1 tablespoon freshly grated horseradish

1 teaspoon Worcestershire sauce

1 teaspoon hot sauce, such as Tabasco

1 tablespoon freshly squeezed lemon juice

1 teaspoon celery salt

Freshly ground black pepper, to taste

2 ounces (¼ cup) vodka, preferably Hangar One Organic Chipotle Vodka

1 green olive

1 lemon wedge

1 pickled pepper

Combine the tomato juice, horseradish, Worcestershire sauce, hot sauce, lemon juice, celery salt and black pepper in a cocktail shaker. Add the vodka and some ice cubes to the shaker. Shake well and strain over an ice-filled soda glass.

Thread the olive, lemon wedge and pickled pepper onto a skewer and garnish the drink.

JERSEY LIGHTNING

Applejack, a blend of apple brandy and pure neutral spirits, has been distilled in southern New Jersey since 1780. The Garden State's apple crop shines in this sweet and spicy cocktail, dreamed up by our general manager Billy Van Dolsen.

MAKES 1 DRINK

1¾ ounces (3½ tablespoons) Laird's New Jersey Apple-jack

1 ounce (2 tablespoons) apple juice

¾ ounce (1½ tablespoons) freshly squeezed lemon juice

½ ounce (1 tablespoon) Ginger Simple Syrup (page 207)

2 ounces (¼ cup) ginger beer, preferably Gosling's

3 thin apple slices

1 piece crystallized ginger

Combine the Applejack, apple juice, lemon juice and simple syrup in a cocktail shaker with ice. Shake then strain into an ice–filled bucket or rocks glass. Top off with the ginger beer. Thread the apple slices and crystallized ginger onto a skewer and garnish.

A WISE CHOICE

The perfect kickoff to a party, this elegant sparkler pairs nicely with rich appetizers like Atlantic Cod Fritters (page 18) and Chicken Liver Mousse (page 29).

MAKES 1 DRINK

1 ounce (2 tablespoons) chilled limoncello

¾ ounce (1½ tablespoons) Housemade Grenadine (page 207)

4 dashes orange bitters

4 ounces (½ cup) sparkling wine, preferably Cava or Prosecco

1 strip orange zest

Add the limoncello, grenadine and bitters to a champage flute. Top off with the sparkling wine and garnish with the strip of orange zest.

AGRICOLA BLOODY MARY   BLOOD ORANGE   GREAT DIRT ROAD MARTINI

PISCO PEAR SOUR   JERSEY LIGHTNING   A WISE CHOICE

BLOOD ORANGE OLD FASHIONED

We prefer to use a single ice ball for our old fashioned; the large mass melts more slowly than smaller cubes, which keeps the drink from getting diluted too quickly.

MAKES 1 DRINK

1 (¼-inch) slice blood orange
1 brandied cherry
1 brown sugar cube
2 dashes Angostura bitters
2 ounces (¼ cup) rye whiskey
½ ounce (1 tablespoon) club soda

Place the blood orange slice, brandied cherry, sugar cube and bitters in a rocks glass. Muddle the ingredients until the sugar cube has dissolved. Add the rye, club soda and ice. Stir to combine.

PISCO PEAR SOUR

Pisco is a potent South American brandy distilled from Muscat grapes. Pear-scented eau de vie and Velvet Falernum—a Caribbean liqueur infused with lime and spices—are unorthodox but delicious additions to a pisco sour. This cocktail isn't complete without the egg white—when shaken, it's what gives this drink its distinctive frothy head.

MAKES 1 DRINK

¾ ounce (1½ tablespoons) pisco
¾ ounce (1½ tablespoons) Poire William eau de vie
¾ ounce (1½ tablespoons) Velvet Falernum liqueur
½ ounce (1 tablespoon) freshly squeezed lime juice
½ ounce (1 tablespoon) Basic Simple Syrup (page 207)
1 large egg white
2 dashes Angostura bitters

Combine all ingredients but the bitters in a cocktail shaker and vigorously shake the mixture without ice. Add ice and shake again. Strain the drink into a chilled coupe or martini glass and sprinkle the bitters onto the froth.

PISCO PEAR SOUR

ICE PICK

At Agricola, we make a raspberry-infused vodka for our take on this classic summer cooler. To do so, crush 4 ounces fresh ripe raspberries and stir them into one 750-ml bottle of vodka. Set the mixture aside in a cool, dark place for 2 weeks to infuse. When the vodka is ready, strain it through a fine-mesh sieve before storing in the cleaned vodka bottle.

SERVES 6

18 ounces (2¼ cups) unsweetened black tea, chilled

12 ounces (1½ cups) raspberry-infused vodka, home-
made or Hangar One

6 ounces (¾ cup) freshly
squeezed lemon juice

6 ounces (¾ cup) Mint Simple
Syrup (page 207)

3 ounces (6 tablespoons)
Domaine de Canton ginger
liqueur

6 pieces crystallized ginger

6 mint sprigs

Combine the iced tea, vodka, lemon juice, mint simple syrup and ginger liqueur in a pitcher with ice. Stir well to combine and pour into Collins glasses. Garnish each drink with a piece of crystallized ginger and a mint sprig.

AUTUMN APPLE SODA

The spiced simple syrup used in this apple soda also works deliciously as a sweetener for a hot toddy or iced tea.

MAKES 1 DRINK

4 ounces (½ cup) apple cider

¾ ounce (1½ tablespoons)
Fall Spice Simple Syrup
[page 207]

4 ounces (½ cup) club soda

1 cinnamon stick, for grating

2 thin apple slices

Combine the apple cider and simple syrup, shake with ice and pour into a Collins glass. Top off with club soda and stir to combine. Grate some cinnamon over the top of the drink and garnish with the apple slices.

STRAWBERRY-BASIL LEMONADE

This is one of our most popular warm-weather coolers—like drinking June in a glass. For a tipsy version, add a slug of vodka or gin.

SERVES 4

8 ripe strawberries, hulled and sliced
1 cup Basil Simple Syrup (page 207)
4 cups cold water
¾ cup freshly squeezed lemon juice

Put the strawberries and basil simple syrup in a pitcher. Using a wooden spoon, muddle the strawberries until completely crushed. Add the water, lemon juice and a large handful of ice cubes. Stir well and pour directly, without straining, into tall glasses.

GRAPEFRUIT-ROSEMARY SODA

In Agricola's kitchen, we almost always prefer the robust depth of Grade B maple syrup to the golden sweetness of Grade A. Surprisingly, maple syrup is a prized crop in New Jersey, thanks to a handful of sugarbush farms in the northern part of the state, though most of what's produced is sold locally.

MAKES 1 DRINK

2 ounces (¼ cup) freshly squeezed grapefruit juice
¾ ounce (1½ tablespoons) maple syrup
Leaves from ¼ sprig rosemary
4 ounces (½ cup) club soda

Combine the grapefruit juice, maple syrup and rosemary leaves in a cocktail shaker with ice. Shake vigorously then pour with ice into a Collins glass. Top off with the club soda and stir to combine.

HOUSEMADE GRENADINE

Many store-bought grenadines are nothing but corn syrup and food coloring, which seems silly when making your own takes all of 5 minutes, and the result tastes so vibrant and complex.

MAKES ABOUT 2½ CUPS

2 cups unsweetened pome-
 granate juice, preferably
 freshly juiced
2 cups packed light brown
 sugar

¼ cup pomegranate molasses
1 tablespoon orange blossom
 water

Put the pomegranate juice in a saucepan and bring to a gentle simmer over moderate heat. Add the brown sugar and stir until dissolved. Remove from the heat and stir in the pomegranate molasses and orange blossom water. Let cool. The grenadine will keep, refrigerated, up to 1 month.

BASIC SIMPLE SYRUP

Our bar is always stocked with a variety of simple syrups, infused with spices and fresh herbs, which add a sweet dimension to many cocktails and nonalcoholic drinks. Follow the basic formula below and then have fun experimenting with your own flavor combinations. If you want to make bigger batches, simply double or triple the recipe. Store the syrups in airtight containers in the refrigerator; they will keep up to 2 weeks.

MAKES ABOUT 1 CUP

1 cup water   1 cup granulated sugar

Heat the water in a small saucepan over moderate heat and bring to a simmer. Add the sugar and stir until it is completely dissolved and the liquid is clear. Remove from the heat and let cool completely.

FALL SPICE SIMPLE SYRUP: Put 2 star anise pods, 2 cinnamon sticks, 2 whole nutmegs and 5 whole cloves in a small sauté pan and toast, stirring, over moderate heat until very fragrant, about 1½ minutes. Remove from the heat. Heat the water and sugar as noted above. Remove from the heat and stir in the toasted spices. Let cool completely, then strain the syrup through a fine-mesh sieve.

GINGER SIMPLE SYRUP: Peel 4 ounces fresh ginger and cut into ½-inch chunks. Heat the water and sugar as noted above. Remove from the heat and stir in the ginger. Let cool completely, then strain the syrup through a fine-mesh sieve.

BASIL SIMPLE SYRUP: Heat the water and sugar as noted above. Remove from the heat and stir in 40 fresh basil leaves. Let cool completely, then strain the syrup through a fine-mesh sieve.

MINT SIMPLE SYRUP: Heat the water and sugar as noted above. Remove from the heat and stir in ½ cup fresh mint leaves (stems discarded). Let cool completely, then strain the syrup through a fine-mesh sieve.

ACKNOWLEDGMENTS

Thanks Ann for coping with me, your serial entrepreneur, filling the voids I left while chasing the next thing. James, Peter and Henry, eat at Agricola, don't ever open a restaurant!

Thanks Mom and Dad, Mary Ellen, Sally, Julie, Ann Marie and Maureen (yes, I have five sisters!). To Rich, Mary Ellen, Kathy, Billy, Josh, Manlee, Steve, Sanaa, you know I like working with a team, and you are the best--the reason Agricola opens each day for business. Thank you Sarah for having sweetened Agricola while you were with us. Thanks chef Michelle for your care and counsel. To all who work with me at Agricola, thank you. Buz, Janet, Kate, Guy and the cookbook team, I appreciate that your years of experience and keen eye for authenticity and quality have been cast on Agricola.

Thank you ICE, Julia, Vince, Frank, Fabiola, David, Roberta, Mateo, Andrew, Erica, Mike, Dan, Charlie, Jeff, Marty. And thank you Phil.

Thanks to the Princeton community for embracing Agricola, making it a place where you can share good times with family and friends. I hope we can be there for you as a stage for your special moments for many years to come.

JIM NAWN
Agricola Proprietor

To the crews of Agricola and Great Road Farm past and present, my deep gratitude for clocking in every day and for your tireless dedication. To Janet and Buz, publishers at Burgess Lea Press, thank you for taking the chance on our little restaurant in Princeton. To Kate, for making sense of a crazy chef, asking the right questions and working so hard to ensure that everything in this book is accurate. To Guy, for your amazing eye; your pictures are worth a thousand tastes. To Farmer Steven, thank you for the hard work and all the dirty candy.

Several people have helped shape my point of view as a chef: George Mahaffey, who gave me the chance; Jeff Jake, for his generosity as a friend and mentor; Alice Waters, for her friendship; Thomas Keller, for inspiring me in ways I never thought possible; and Manlee Siu, my chef de cuisine for the past six years on two coasts—you motivate me every day with your ability and continued pursuit of excellence.

To the diners at Agricola who have not only become loyal guests but great friends, who give us the enthusiasm and criticism we need to change and grow, thank you for spending your time with us.

To Jim and Ann, my thanks for your steadfast support and friendship. To my mom and dad, you guys helped turn a spark into a rewarding profession, and I owe it all to you both. And to especially my incredible partner in life, my wife Sarah, for years of support. I can never thank you enough for the strength you give me every day.

JOSH THOMSEN
Executive Chef

I would not be able to do this work of farming without encouragement from my wife Robin. My son Van Pelt reminds me every day that we need a healthy ecosystem for the future.

Jim and Ann Nawn, you have believed in me and given me an amazing opportunity to manage a farm and beyond. Thank you Manlee, Josh, Peter, Jason, Fito, Billy, Lauren, Rich, Kathy, Mary Ellen and everyone who keeps Agricola running. It was a pleasure to work with Kate, Guy, Buz and Janet who came to us with an idea for a cookbook and turned it into reality.

Farming is best learned by doing and I am in debt to Tom and Trish of Blooming Glen Farm and Mike from North Slope Farm. A big thank you to the Great Road Farm crew past and present: Sam, Andrew, Kyle, and Annie. We have worked together in the trenches and you are vital to our operation. Thank you Mom and Dad for giving me the tools to be independent and resourceful, and teaching me to always trust my gut. Ryan, Lisa, Lindsay and Paul, I hope you keep eating all the kale I bring to our family get-togethers. I love you all.

STEVEN TOMLINSON
Farmer, Great Road Farm

SOURCES

GREAT ROAD FARM
Skillman, NJ
greatroadfarm.com
Our own farm provides not just to
Agricola but to farmers markets in
New Jersey and New York City. CSA
members pick up their shares at the
restaurant.

ACME SMOKED FISH
Brooklyn, NY
acmesmokedfish.com
Smoked whitefish and other delicacies
from the sea.

CASTLE VALLEY MILL
Doylestown, PA
castlevalleymill.com
Stoneground wheat, spelt, cornmeal
and more.

CHERRY GROVE FARM
Lawrenceville, NJ
cherrygrovefarm.com
Organic cheeses plus sustainably raised
pork, lamb and eggs.

CRESCENT DUCK
Aquebogue, NY
crescentduck.com
This fifth-generation family farm
supplies us with superb Long Island
ducks.

D'ARTAGNAN
Newark, NJ
Dartagnan.com
Our source for naturally raised rabbit
and guinea hen.

GRIGGSTOWN FARM
Princeton, NJ
griggstown.com
Well-known all over the tri-state area
for their quail, pheasants, turkeys,
chickens and poussins.

**HUDSON VALLEY
FOIE GRAS**
Ferndale, NY
hudsonvalleyfoiegras.com
A trusted source for humanely
produced foie gras.

**LANCASTER FARM
FRESH COOPERATIVE**
Leola, PA
lancasterfarmfresh.com
This Lancaster County farming coop
supplies us with pasture-raised eggs,
milk and butter.

**MAINE SEA SALT
COMPANY**
Marshfield, ME
maineseasalt.com
In our opinion, the best domestic sea
salt you can find.

MAX & ME
Carversville, PA
maxhansensmokedsalmon.com
No one knows salmon better than Max.

MILLBROOK VENISON
Millbrook, NY
845-677-8457
Our choice for domestic venison.

PARADISE HILL FARM
Vincentown, NJ
609-859-9701
This farm near the Pine Barrens is
a great source for cranberries and
blueberries.

**PAT LAFRIEDA
MEAT PURVEYORS**
North Bergen, NJ
lafrieda.com
Exclusive distributors of Creekstone
Farm beef from small family farms.

POLYSCIENCE
Torrance, CA
polyscienceculinary.com
Sous vide technology allows us to serve
perfectly cooked meat, poultry and fish
every time.

RIDGE VALLEY FARMS
Green Lane, PA
suejimmyers@verizon.net
Jim and Sue Myers produce the
excellent maple syrup we use.

ROJO'S ROASTERY
Lambertville, NJ
rojosroastery.com
Perfectly roasted coffee beans from
24 countries, plus coffeemaking
equipment.

SAMUELS & SON SEAFOOD
Philadelphia, PA
samuelsandsonseafood.com
Our impeccable source for local
seafood.

SHIBUMI FARM
Princeton, NJ
shibumifarm.com
Cultivated specialty mushrooms.

TASSOT APIARIES
Milford, NJ
tassotapiaries.com
High-quality local New Jersey honey.

TERHUNE ORCHARDS
Princeton, NJ
terhuneorchards.com
Many varieties of apples.

VALLEY SHEPHERD
CREAMERY
Long Valley, NJ
valleyshepherd.com
Artisanal cheeses made from grazed
sheep, goat and cow milk.

ZONE 7
Ringoes, NJ
freshfromzone7.com
The linchpin in our local farm to table
movement delivers food from the farms
straight to the chefs.

SEED SOURCES

BAKER CREEK HEIRLOOM
SEEDS
rareseeds.com
Blue, green, orange, striped and white
heirloom tomatoes, plus many carrot
varieties.

FEDCO SEEDS
fedcoseeds.com
Carrots, turnips, onions, potatoes,
peppers.

HIGH MOWING ORGANIC
SEEDS
highmowingseeds.com
Cabbage, celery, hot pepper, basil.

JOHNNY'S SELECTED
SEEDS
johnnyseeds.com
Lettuce, arugula, winter squash, flowers,
peppers, tomatoes, leeks and more

SOUTHERN EXPOSURE
SEED EXCHANGE
southernexposure.com
Heirloom tomatoes from Arkansas
Traveler to Wins All Cherry

TURTLE TREE SEED
turtletreeseed.org
Some interesting varieties of kale,
including Delaway and Judy's

WILD GARDEN SEED
wildgardenseed.com
Escarole varieties including Blonde
Full-Hearted and Anjou, plus
85 different lettuces.

INDEX